SEDUCTION

OF THE MIND

A PILGRIMAGE OF SPIRIT

NITA GOYAL

Seduction of the Mind

Robertson Publishing
59 N. Santa Cruz Avenue, Suite B
Los Gatos, California 95030 USA
888) 354-5957 · www.RobertsonPublishing.com

Dedicated to (Ratan Guruji) Guruji. His presence in my life has made it sublime.

CONTENTS

PART 1

PART 2

PART 3

PART 4

PREFACE

If I think about the beginning of the book it takes me five year back when I began writing random thoughts to express myself. My intention was to simply express what was going on in the mind and explore where it would lead to. Little did I know that it would take me on the most adventurous ride of my life. As I believe that everything in life is effortless, and so the thoughts came and words were formed effortlessly.

The first real foundation of the book was set even years earlier when I was still a child. I have mentioned the fateful day as the day I met the beggar and the same day I felt betrayed by the Universe. As a child I often found myself wondering about eternal questions like who am I? How everything works? There was a huge world standing in front of me, how did it even come into being? I saw my parents go to temples, worship various idols, perform various rituals in the name of religion. It always perplexed me. When I asked them about God, their answers could not satisfy my curious mind. As I grew older more questions came, but without answers. I stopped thinking about them due to demands of growing up.

In the spring of 2005, suddenly in a flash I experienced something immense and my life had not remained the same since. It shook the foundation on which my mind stood and carried with itself all previous concepts, ideas, and conditioning. From there on my real journey began. My perception shifted and I began to understand things in a totally different way. Call it insight, call it understanding, or call it revelations. I call them flashes of intelligence which though began as flashes but soon turned into waves and waves of intellectual illuminations. I began writing such staggering thoughts. More I contemplated, more I wrote, and more it became clearer and clearer. My doubts vanished as if they didn't exist in the first place.

I became excited to share the amazing knowledge with the world. I found something precious and wanted others to experience as well. It was a calling; something I was propelled to do. In the process of writing I was helping myself grow and evolve to new possibilities and heights. The book started as a personal story but somewhere in the middle became universal. I ceased to exist and what remained was spiritual adventure. I asked questions, I got answers. I became my own student and my own master.

In a humble endeavor to express the wonderful knowledge which I have stumbled upon, I present it in the form of a book through conversation in between three characters. I deeply believe that the ideas and thoughts expressed are not mine but have come through me. I have been used as an instrument of expression of forces bigger than myself, though the action of writing has been initiated by me. I would be a fool to think that I could singlehandedly produce this book without the universal force behind me. I do not even consider it written by me. Who am I... just a drop of water, but I also accept humbly that an entire ocean is behind a drop of water. I know in my heart that collective consciousness is supporting me at every step of the way, propelling me to go forward. I know this because when I write, I plan on writing something but soon new thoughts immerge without thinking. Thoughts I could never have thought myself. Effortlessly I would write for hours, thoughts would come, words would form. I would read my words as if I am reading someone else's words; I would be inspired by them.

My writings are influenced by the words I have heard through the mouth of my Guruji, who resides in India and also through writings of many wise people including Osho, Swami Krishnananda, J. Krishanamurti, Swami Vivekananda and Shri Ramakrishna Paramhamsa, and my own insights and experiences. Ancient eastern texts Yoga Vasistha and various Upanisads have also deeply influenced my thoughts and consequent insights. At places it may seem that the words are the same as discussed by these great minds. Their effect is profound on my thought process and such words have been embedded in my mind so much that it is hard for me to distinguish if I am writing the words or I have heard them so many times that they are embedded in my subconscious. I acknowledge such great words from such great minds.

I hope readers find support, help, and inspiration to lead enriching and harmonious lives. Just the way it has helped me, may it also help other; this is my prayer.

Nita Goyal

ACNOWLEDGMENTS

I thank Guruji from the bottom of my heart. Words cannot suffice the gratitude I feel for him. It is a communication without speech. Words diminish the gratitude and love.

I thank my family for their patience, love, and also believing in me. Their love has kept me sane in challenging times. I thank them for being there for me when I was not there for them. My children, my husband, without their support this book may not have been possible. I thank my parents for their love and support, and my extended family and friends for being there for me. Thank you all.

I extend my gratitude to all the people who have touched my life and all those whom I have not met, not yet. I thank all the masters and teachers of the world who came and gave to the world the most precious thing, knowledge. I thank all the authors of the world for writing what they wrote and enriching the world with their words. I thank all the scientists, who gave to the world a beautiful thing, the thirst for knowledge. Their inquiry, observation, and experimentation gave all of us the most wonderful thing, a quest to reach to the bottom of the things or to the beginning.

I thank Gail for giving her input for editing the manuscript. I thank Alicia at publishers for her patience and helpful advice.

Finally, I acknowledge the divine in me and I acknowledge the divine in you, and I acknowledge the divine in the space between me and you.

It all began with a simple, yet profound question: Who am I?

PART ONE

Your heart knows in silence the secrets

of the days and the nights.

But your ears thirst for the sound

of your hearts knowledge.

You would know in words

that which you have always known in thought.

You would touch with your fingers

the naked body of your dreams.

And the treasure of your infinite depths

would be revealed to your eyes.

But let there be no scales to weigh

your unknown treasure;

And seek not the depth of your knowledge

With staff or sounding line.

For self is a sea boundless and measureless.

-*Khalil Gibran*

≈ 1 ≈

The Beginning

"The same stream of life that runs through my veins night and day runs through the world and dances in rhythmic measures. It is the same life that shoots in joy through the dust of the earth in numberless blades of grass and breaks into tumultuous waves of leaves and flowers. It is the same life that is rocked in the ocean-cradle of birth and of death, in ebb and in flow. I feel my limbs are made glorious by the touch of this world of life and my pride is from the life-throb of ages dancing in my blood this moment." —Rabindranath Tagore

Radha stood at the peak of the mountain admiring the sun rising from behind the horizon. The whole sky was turning orange. It was a magnificent sight. She could see the sun and the sky with its indescribable splendor *and* she could hear the sounds of morning traffic in the background. But, for now the sound of sky with its profound depth was there. It was the sound of beauty and presence, loud and sharp. She was filled with delight—it was intoxicating. In no time, the whole sky was lit up by the sun which stood in its own glory... naked, intense, and proud. The sky's majestic beauty never failed to astound her. She marveled at the fact that the sky was always changing but always there—the day she was born, when she was one, five, fourteen...looking after her, loving her.

Love enveloped her as tears welled up in her eyes. Her whole being was exploding with joy. Nobody was paying attention to the sky. She wanted to shake everybody out of their slumber, make them see the beauty of existence and the abundance of love all around; love which was everywhere for them to feel and celebrate. She marveled at the cleverness of the mind and its force on humans that the most profound and magical was missed, in plain sight.

Not long ago, she had wondered about life and its purpose. Her days were filled with contemplation on eternal questions and nights tormented her with restlessness. Little did she know that she was embarking on a journey too adventurous to even think about, that it would take her to wonders of astonishing new heights. Once more, she looked around and saw beauty everywhere...the beauty of existence, of each and every tree, flower, and of every blade of grass—astonishingly intelligent and breathtakingly beautiful. How the same beauty and intelligence had harassed her for so many years. How restless she had become.

Who am I? Who are we? How do we find ourselves in this world seemingly coming from of nowhere, and yet never raising a question as to our origin?

These were not sudden question. She had often found herself wondering about them as far back—as she could remember. Was she just a physical form? That couldn't be right, because her features, her body were somehow genetically produced. If she had different set of parents, she could have had a different face, even a different gender. She could have been a bird or a tree. What decided that she was to be Radha with that particular set of appearance and personality? Her name was just a name made up by her parents. She could as well be named anything else.

Her first memory of such wondering was—when she was three years old and looked into a mirror. She was at once startled and fascinated by her reflection. Oh, what joy! She wanted to touch her reflection, but all she could touch was a wall of glass. She wished she could talk to that image of her, play with it, but it was elusive. She wondered what was her physical body—something as science knows it, or was it something else altogether...a mystery and a marvel. After that she could never look at a face and not be overwhelmed with awe and wonder. Everyone was more than a body and yet felt bound by it. It was a clever and a necessary tool to experience the world. But the question remained unanswered as to the cause of the body.

Questions never left her though it seemed that she ignored them, succumbing to the immediate demands of growing up and the pressure of dealing with the world. Like an ignored child craving for attention, the unanswered questions hammered her again and again till she could ignore them no more. Eventually answers began to come in the most inexplicable ways—through mysterious channels—which defied logic but stood as a fact. She became aware of a higher dimension existing parallely. This dimension was always there, untainted by any thought or action, but since her mind was preoccupied with the things of the world, she didn't recognize it earlier.

≈ **2** ≈

Dynamics of Free-will and Karma

"As I gaze on your face, mystery overwhelms me; you who belong to all have become mine. What magic has snared the world's treasure in these slender arms of mine?" —Rabindranath Tagore

TWO YEARS EARLIER

Radha woke up frightened and amazed. She had slept peacefully that night thinking about her two beautiful children, Abhi and Anya. It was their fifth birthday, and she and Suraj had celebrated it with pomp.

She remembered how fascinated she was when she found out that she was going to have twins. It was such a warm feeling. Her body was forming two new people. She felt the power and magic of the powerful and the magical. Her days were filled with wonder at experiencing the ways of nature. Why it was thought to be a regular day to day thing... Something much deeper and grander than biology was going on when a body reproduced. How a life was created from the fusion of cells was in itself intriguing and enigmatic. She became aware of a presence in her body, intelligent and aware presence.

She wondered: From the beginning of time one thing is observed to be common in nature—from plants to animals to humans—to reproduce and multiply. This intelligence is prevalent everywhere and in all times. *From one cell came many.* This need to reproduce has created such varied life in the cosmos. From where are the cells getting instruction to multiply? Isn't it inherent in them like a program? I may perish in the process of time, but Life cannot be extinguished. It makes me eternal. My mind cannot think like that. My mind does not know what to think.

Radha's heart was filled with love for someone—two people— who were not even born. It was a spiritual experience. The unborn were not just hers but part of something more...a phenomenon...vast and mysterious, greater and beyond human understanding. Mystery enveloped her like the wind caresses a flower, cherished her like a mother cherishes a child. Two other minds were getting encircled in a body to create, express, and experience. She was part of the phenomenon, a big part. She felt proud. She was been used to set a stage for two soul to come and experience life. She realized it was possible for different people to be merged without any separateness. It was the beginning of life—baby and Mother.

When the twins were born, she looked at them in wonder. Her throat would choke up and her mind would go numb whenever she thought of them. She could feel her own splendor whenever the twins looked at her. Their small fragile bodies looked like they were going to break any moment, and yet they were so strong sustained by an unknown force. She marveled at the enormous power such tiny beings held in the dot of their hearts. In their presence, everything ceased to exist, even her. For a long time, only love remained. It overwhelmed her.

She wondered: Where they were a year ago before been born to me...Were they living somewhere in far off land I know nothing about...What else could be more wonderful, more powerful than a baby. It carries a force that cannot be subdued. Put a baby in a savage's hand and watch how he changes. All menacing force melts in front of a tiny defenseless baby. There is nothing ordinary about the birth of a child. At once I became aware that I am capable of loving someone so much more than I'd realized. Love is a powerful force that drives the whole world. No matter how much my mind thinks or my intellect analyses, it cannot transport me to oneness. I am spontaneously transported into these magnificent realms. This shows these realms do exist where I am whole and blissful without an effort whatsoever.

That night, Radha was surprised when she saw a face from the past—or was it a dream? The face had the glow of angels—not that she had seen any angels. It radiated with an angelic brilliance, certainly not human. She remembered the face. It had persisted in her memory since childhood. It was not a happy memory.

It was the face of a beggar encountered on a random street on a random day, an unforgettable day, and the day she felt betrayed and became fearful of God. She was eight years old. She had gone to the temple with her parents when a beggar came and asked for money. He hadn't eaten in two days, so he said. She could not forget those eyes. They had lingered in her memories even after two decades, eyes deep with sorrow, hunger, and helplessness. They gave her shudders. He must have been her father's age.

As a child, she wondered why God made him like that. If God loved everybody the same, then why had [1]He given him misery and her family good luck. She felt guilt and shame. Maybe she was taking the beggar's share. She had everything: food, clothes, and friends. He had none. She was enjoying her life. God loved her more, so He gave her more. Strange unpleasant emotions possessed her, guilt, shame, and fear all rolled in one. Guilt that she was taking his share, shame that she had more than him, fear that if she did not give him money then it would be taken from her.

God did not love everybody the same, she concluded. That meant she could offend God. He was not all love and beauty. There was ugliness in the world too which He created. She felt betrayed by life, followed by immense fear. After coming home that day, she sat sadly in her room and watched helplessly as fear possessed her, filled her from top to the bottom. She prayed not to make her like the beggar, bestow on her good luck. Deep in her heart she knew she had already become what she was scared of. She had become the beggar. That night she had gone and slept by her mother's side. Intense love was radiating from her mother's arm. Everything was all right in her arms. She would protect Radha from God's wrath.

---

[1] Due to the difficulty in expression, God is referred as He. It does not in any way suggest that God is a male.

Radha was surprised, after so many years she remembered the face. Why was she dreaming of the beggar now? Suddenly she felt hungry. She went in the kitchen and fixed herself a sandwich. Once she had eaten, she went to check on the twins. They were fast asleep. They looked so innocent. She felt lucky to have them in her life. She came back and slept by Suraj's side.

The beggar was still there, waiting, as she slept. His eyes shone with unknown compassion and intelligence.

"Ask what it is that you want to know," the beggar said.

A strange kind of calmness descended on Radha. She remembered her guilt accompanied by shame and many times she visited the orphanage to help the children. It offered no answers. She experienced more mental turmoil instead of eradicating the guilt, and she failed to understand why there was misery in the world. She was not helping kids due to compassion, but because she felt compelled to do it. It made her feel like the culprit and victim at the same time.

"Why are you here?" she asked.

"You invited me," he replied calmly.

It seemed the most natural thing to hear.

"Why are some people prosperous and some poor? Why some people successful and some not? Why this difference if everyone is same to God?" She asked the questions that had tormented her for two decades.

He looked at her intensely. She could not interpret his peculiar gaze.

"When we travel from one place to another some people go by foot, some by bus, some by train, and some by airplane depending on their capabilities and resources, and also their wishes. Even within one source of transportation there are various categories like economy, business, and first class suiting everyone's need. Different people are given different stations in life according to their wishes, thoughts, actions, and capabilities," he answered tenderly.

His face was becoming more and more radiant.

Why he didn't age a day, Radha wondered.

"But why would someone go by foot if one can go by airplane?"

"Some people can afford first class airplane ticket, but they might still choose to go by train just for the experience," he said.

"Still, it seems silly. Why anyone would like to experience poverty just for the experience. Everyone knows it is not a nice experience."

"How do you know it is not a nice experience? You can have knowledge of things you have experienced. Suppose you want to see Niagara Falls. No matter how much you have heard about it and seen the photographs, it is nothing compared to actual experience of being there and seeing with your own eyes. There are as many experiences as there are desires and wishes. Traveling by bus is a totally different adventure than by airplane. Some minds like the adventure," the beggar clarified.

"Sometimes people live in miserable conditions. It cannot be their choice. They are born into such situations. What do you say about people with serious handicaps or financial failures beyond their control?" she asked.

"What about them? Have you not seen people rise above their situations? History is full of such people who refused to let their circumstances limit them. The culprit is not fate but our own lack of belief in the fact that we are unlimited. Such circumstances are put there for us to grow and evolve. We cannot learn to swim if there is no water," he answered calmly.

Radha asked further, "What about terrible things happening to good people all the time? What about people losing everything in an earthquake or tsunami or being a victim of terrorist attack? What about hundreds of meaningless deaths every day all around the world?"

His face gleamed in moonlight, having a perfectly calm expression. "There is nothing meaningless in creation," he said, "things can happen to us that seem terrible at the time, but always remember they are part of the grander plan. Horrible things can happen, but they are necessary for our evolution, to go to the next level."

A powerful emotion rose in Radha.

"Do you mean blessings in disguise?"

"You can choose to say whatever you want. These are words. Everything is planned on a grander dimension which is at the background of our existence. It is the foundation of our being but we ignore it, self-possessed by arrogance. There is a story of an ordinary person doing the same thing every day, day after day for months and years: raising a family, having a career, indulging in friends and family. When things happened the way he wanted, he was happy and when not, he would be sad. He was always living in the future: imagining and planning what life would be in a few years. Present was just a passing block. The world had become mundane to him. He started questioning the purpose of life and existence. One day a holy person passed by. He felt his restlessness and told him that he was part of a beautiful tapestry called the universe, so was everyone else. Though he felt he was doing nothing, he was a link in the chain of world order. If he stopped what he was doing, it would create a break in the chain and everything would collapse. Everyone would be affected including seemingly important people of the world, since everyone was linked in the chain without a beginning or an end. Nobody was trifle in the world and nothing futile. What seemed mundane was magical; the ordinary was, in truth, extraordinary. From the rising of the sun to the flight of the birds, from the elegance of the trees to the flow of the rivers, everything was magical. When he smiled, the universe smiled with him; when he cried, the cosmos shed tears with him."

A deep silence surrounded Radha.

"Why don't I see it?" Radha asked, her voice barely a whisper.

"Imagine a roadway system. You see the road in front of you. If you are flying in a helicopter, you can see the network of roads connecting various towns and cities. If you are flying a little higher in an airplane, a much wider scale of roads are seen. In the same way, you can see the higher—and grander—pattern of life if you can raise your awareness, instead of running after the things of the world in an endeavor to belong and to become. When you begin to live in your own presence, you can take part in the world order consciously. Always remember we are coming from the same place and going to the same place. And we all are in it together."

"But what about countless tragic deaths every day...What can they possibly signify?" she asked frustrated.

"When you travel, you buy ticket to the destination you wish to go to. Why do you blame life or death for your choice of town or city? Life loves you in totality. It does not interfere in your choices. On the way train stops at various stations, and different people enter or exit according to their destinations. Just because a fellow passenger has exited does not mean life has been unfair. It means he (or she) has arrived at the destination. He might board another train or just hang out a while longer enjoying the place. There is a bigger unseen picture. You read meaning into situations and people. You are not grieving for him but at your own loss, because you have grown attached to that person, because you miss that person. In reality, you are traveling and other people are traveling together. That's all. Why are you making so much fuss about it? Just enjoy the journey. Life is meant to enjoy and celebrate. You meet certain people, you form relations, and you make opinions and stories—to make the journey enjoyable. If you become attached to your stories, you cannot blame it on life, or on death."

Radha had so many questions and so little time. She feared he would leave before she had the chance to ask all her questions. She needed more time to clarify her thoughts.

She asked her next question, "Then why are successful people getting more successful and poor people poorer? Why this gap if we all are together?"

The beggar looked at her. It was a simple and profound look, wanting her to understand.

"Look at the sun, look at the rain. Does the sun say, you are poor I am not going to give you sunshine, or does rain fall on successful people's houses and not on poor people's. They do not discriminate. They just do what they do. The sun gives light, heat, and warmth. Rain gives water, abundantly and joyously, without any discrimination. You keep your doors and windows closed, and then complain that life is not fair. Life delights to give you what you want. All you have to do is be open, to receive what the universe has to offer,"

Chills ran through Radha's spine.

The beggar spoke further, "There is an ancient story about lord Krishna and his disciple Arjuna. They were crossing a remote village when Arjuna asked, 'Why are you partial? Why do you give some people everything and some people nothing but misery?' Krishna didn't say a word at that time. After a while they came across a well and decided they would camp there for the night since water was nearby. Lord Krishna commanded Arjuna, 'Arjuna, go and fetch water from the well, and some bricks to support our temporary shelter.' As soon as he went near the well, Arjuna realized there were two wells. One was well maintained with nice rocks and stones, and the other was crumbling from places. Bricks and stones were coming out of its sides. He looked at both wells and decided to take bricks from the ill maintained one since it was already old and crumbling. Nice well looked too nice to be disturbed. Someone must be working hard looking after it. When he came back Lord Krishna was laughing. 'Look, you did the same thing, you hypocrite! You accuse me of being partial, even you did the same. You took bricks from the broken well and left the good one untouched."

A silence ensued. In that silence, an understanding was beginning to take hold in Radha's heart.

The beggar spoke, "This is the law of the universe. Whatever you pay attention to, it grows—success as well as failure. Whatever you work to maintain, it becomes abundant, richness as well as poverty—of the mind or of the possessions. It is like planting a seed. Though a thought, word, or action is one seed, it grows and multiplies, giving abundant fruit. Fruit will be according to the seed planted. If you plant a bitter, angry, and resentful seed, the fruit will also be bitter, angry, and resentful. If you plant kindness, compassion, love, and abundance, the fruit will be kindness, compassion, love, and abundance. You cannot blame life or God for partiality. *They* did nothing. Life just follows the law of nature. It is *you* who plants the seed. You have to be careful what you plant. Plant well, my friend, for one day the tree will grow and you will enjoy its fruit, whether you like it or not. No matter how many candles you burn, how many rituals you perform, or how many prayers you recite, a seed of the Neem tree (it has bitter leaves) cannot grow into an Apple tree."

"Karma, the law of nature...," Radha mustered enough courage to say.

"You can call it anything you want. These are just words. Understanding the phenomenon is important; otherwise, you will be caught in the web of words like a fly is caught in a spider's web." He looked at Radha intensely and continued, "For every action there is an equal and opposite reaction. Karma is the reaction set up by the cosmic forces exactly in proportion to your—an individual's—action."

"When you smile at your neighbor; what happens?" He asked after a slight pause.

"He smiles back at me."

"And when you resent him?"

"He resents me," Radha smiled as the meaning sank into her.

"World is a mirror in which you see your own reflection. If you smile, the world smiles at you. If you get angry, the whole world will get angry at you. The mirror does not lie; it simply reflects—the good, the bad, and the ugly."

"This is fascinating."

"If your actions are negative—in thoughts, words, or in actual physical terms—you don't have to wait for the judgment day, and neither do you have to be in hell in after-life. You will bear the consequences of your actions in this very same life. When anger strikes you, *you* are its first victim. *You* are the one who feels the wrath of anger before anyone else. If you resent someone, *you* are the first one who feels the negativity. This is a tremendous truth."

A great silence fell between them as Radha tried to recapitulate.

"There is an amazing story explaining the elegance and intricacy of action and reaction," he continued. "In a farming community in India, two brothers inherited the family farm. It so happened, one brother suddenly died in an accident. The other brother, in his greed, murdered his brother's wife and dumped her body in deep forest. Everyone thought she had run away. The brother became the sole owner of a vast farmland, and led a happy and luxurious life with his wife and children. After ten years, he had to go to some other city where no one knew him. One night a woman abruptly came in front of his car. He stopped to help and realized that she had been stabbed and was bleeding to death. In an effort to ease her pain he took the knife out, and at the very same moment police arrived. Seeing him with the body and the murder weapon, they arrested him. He hired expensive lawyers and spent all his money for his defense. Finally he was convicted and given a death penalty. The day he was to be hanged he said that the punishment was fair, he deserved it. Even though he didn't murder that woman, he certainly committed the crime of killing someone at some other time and place."

The beggar smiled and then laughed. His laughter filled the air.

"An action always creates, however small or insignificant it may be, and you will live through the reaction, however pleasant or unpleasant it may be. This is an infallible system. Your thoughts are potent, because, ultimately, your thoughts will manifest into your actions. You have to be careful what you create: joy or fear, love or hatred, abundance or poverty—mental as well as material. Remember that your consciousness is your action. Spontaneous reactions are taking place in the cosmos whenever you feel, think, speak, or act, because for every action..."

"...there is an equal and opposite reaction," Radha finished the sentence.

"It is fundamental, because the foundation of your future life is laid in the present moment, from moment to moment."

"This is unbelievable."

"We are related mystically to the world—and to life itself. We are separate and distinct from the world is an original lie on which Creation stands. Just observe how the entire mechanism of our body rises up in the process of digestion as soon as we take a bite of food, even if it is one tiny bite. Same thing happens as soon as we begin to think or act—the entire cosmos rises up in action in the process of cause and effect."

"A physical body is one whole mechanism, I agree, but I don't see how it applies to the entire cosmos," Radha presented her doubts. "I exist as an individual separate and distinct from other individuals, things, and the world,"

He smiled mysteriously. "Let's try one more time. What happens when you walk?"

"I just walk," Radha replied, confused.

"Your legs are not moving independent of you, but you are walking as a whole person through a command issued by the entire organism mind-body complex. If somehow your legs thought themselves to be one whole entity, separate and distinct from the body, they would believe to be walking independently. Similarly, the belief that you are separate and distinct from the world is an error in understanding. There is no such thing as personal or independent activity of any one individual. The entire cosmos vibrates when any action is performed by anyone in any part of the world, even seemingly small acts of eating and walking. Though you believe that your thoughts and actions are private, you can't be further away from the truth. *You are responsible for all and all are responsible for you."*

His face was glowing more and more with each moment.

She listened motionless and became aware of a silence inside her. The silence expanded and spread to every corner of her being as she became more alert and alive.

"To think of it, even science says the same thing," she said, "that events do not take place at particular points in space and time. Wars, earthquakes, hurricanes effecting thousands of people living in specific places actually do not happen there. What is this mystery?"

"It is an agitation of the whole organism manifesting at a certain part," the beggar explained, "A war, a volcano, or an earthquake may be happening in a particular part, but it is engendered by the agitation of the total organism of the world. Science has realized the phenomenal truth of a continuum which is the ultimate reality of the universe. It is pure energy—and energy is not a localized movement. Quantum science has landed the world practically on the doorsteps of the ancient texts saying that all actions are cosmic action."

Radha sat down to collect herself. She was continuously affecting the cosmos by her thoughts, words, and actions—everyone was; just the mere thought gave her chills.

"It is too much of a responsibility. I can't be good all the time," she said.

Radha recognized a faint hint of sadness in his eyes as he said, "No matter how good your actions are they still bind you. The consequences will be good things, but, still, they are consequences. You don't get freedom. On the other hand, you become slave to the pleasures of life."

She looked at him, puzzled.

He spoke further, "The very urge to express individuality is an action. You cannot exist except through action. And in every action there is equal and opposite reaction. You laugh when something good happens and cry when something bad happens. They built you—and destroy you."

"There has to be a way out."

"It will lose its grip on you if you act out of love, joy, and compassion rather than expecting a return."

"Work for work's sake," Radha muttered.

"Yes. When you expect a return from your action, then you are bound by Karma."

"Everyone works for a purpose. It is called goal. You are saying it is wrong? If I expect nothing from work, why should I work at all?" Radha asked.

The beggar looked at her as if he had a deep ache in his heart, for not been able to convey the simplest thing.

"Joy itself is the motivation. Work for the joy of working. There are few moments in playing a game when you are totally engrossed in it—not worried about winning or losing. You are there with your whole presence, enjoying. That is the aim of life too. If you can act without any motivation other than joy in your daily life, then all your actions will be great action. Then you can never lose; the universe will fill you with overwhelming happiness and love, and all your ambitions and triumphs will look like child's play.

"Or let's take another example, if you get hurt on your leg—does your hand think why should I put medicine on the leg? Health itself is the fruit. Imagine the world to be a tree and yourself as a leaf on that tree. You are getting nourishment automatically by being part of the tree. You are a part of the whole. If you act for the growth and harmony of the whole, the part is automatically taken care of. Look at the universe. Everything is done for its delight. The sun does not stop shining and rain does not stop falling. They act spontaneously. Everything in the universe—except human—is working not for any reason but for the joy of working. This is a fundamental truth. You feel you are an outsider to the world because you treat the world as an outsider."

"Treat others as you would like to be treated. Treat your neighbor with love whether you know him or not..." Radha mumbled under her breath.

The beggar said, "If you can act with the understanding that you are an instrument through which the cosmic forces work notwithstanding the fact that you have initiated the action individually, it will be a great action."

"The very thought is unacceptable," Radha mused. "This is disempowerment. It means I have no free will, I am only a puppet in the hands of God or the universe."

"Again, you do not understand your relationship with God — Universe. It is preposterous for you to think that there is an organic living connection between you and the universe. Understand the great truth of your identity with the atmosphere you live in," he said, his eyes shining like the sun. "You are an integral part of God. What you do, God does; what God does, you do. What freedom does a cell in your body have, and yet without that cell the body cannot function. Your body is only an organized structure of billions and billions of cells. Why is it hard for you to comprehend that you are a cell in the body of the universe. God is a name given to *Consciousness* inhabiting the universe. What will you tell a seed that it has no free will, and yet it is a reservoir of such a magnificent structure, the tree."

Sunlight was shining on a dewdrop reflecting brilliance of colors. It attracted Radha's attention and filled her heart with delight. The beggar saw it too. "You are a single color in the whole spectrum of light, and God is white light. Where is white light if even one color is missing? White light is made of different colors. If there were no colors, there would be no light. Don't you see how powerful you are — everyone is? God needs you for creation."

Tears rolled down Radha's eyes on hearing the holy truth.

"Where do you live?" the beggar asked after a moment.

"Delhi," Radha replied.

"If you say you live in India or on planet Earth, you won't be wrong. Stretching the imagination further, you are in the Solar System, the Milky Way galaxy, finally in the universe. The universe is such a staggering word because it denotes immensity and vastness. You may feel you are just a speck, but look what a speck you are. Without you, the universe won't exist the way it does. If you were a mere drop of water, what is the ocean made of but drops of water — billions and trillions drops of water. What action does water perform except being fluid! If it were not fluid, it wouldn't be water. It would be something but not water. Does water need a purpose or freedom to be wet—or does it need someone's permission to flow."

Radha fell asleep and then came back to dreaming, and she kept seeing the beggar. This went on for a long time. As Radha drifted in and out of sleep, the beggar's words kept resonating in her head: *Does water need someone's permission to flow?*

≈ 3 ≈

Desires Are Holy

"Day by day you are making me worthy of the simple great gifts that you gave to me unasked--this sky and the light, this body and the life and the mind-saving me from perils of overmuch desire. There are times when I languidly linger and times when I awaken and hurry in search of my goal, but cruelly you hid yourself from before me. Day by day you are making me worthy of your full acceptance by refusing me ever and saving me from perils of weak, uncertain desire." —*Rabindranath Tagore*

When Radha woke up at some time after midnight she could not shake off the feeling that the beggar was still there somewhere. Their conversation was not finished. There was so much she wanted to know. She took a sip from a glass of water she always kept at her bedside. She drank the whole glass in one gulp. As she went back to sleep, she wondered: *What about longings in the heart, wishes I want to fulfill? Does that not matter?*

The beggar appeared as soon as she closed her eyes and began to speak tenderly, "Everything matters. That is what makes an individual an individual. Desire is the creative impulse in the universe. A single desire can change the course of rivers. It is sacred; worship it. It is powerful; surrender to it. Whatever you aspire to, you shall attain to. Your longings are intelligent urges that know how to fulfill themselves. They come due to the very nature of your existence in the world. If seen in clear light, you are not asking for things but for your lost being, your true self."

"Ask and it shall be given, knock and the door will be opened," Radha mumbled.

"In truth, the door is always open; it always has been. You move in a direction towards fulfillment of your desires and longings only."

"How...?"

"The universe is governed by a system; it is precise and flawless. The system does not ignore anyone. Every thought has to fulfill itself, if not today then tomorrow. Automatic actions are taking place in the cosmos intending to fulfill a desire, any desire. You can compare the system of the universe to a computer program, except it is self-operating."

"But there are so many wishes."

"There might be viruses in a computer program—or it can be hacked into, but laws governing the system of the universe are exact and inexorable. Preference is given to the strongest thought and feeling. Lesser ones receive attention later on, at the proper time and proper place. You will not be taken to a place that you have not desired, or rather, which does not follow as a natural consequence of your thoughts, feelings, and actions. Your deep seated longings are the strongest thoughts and, therefore, the strongest actions."

"But, not all my desires get fulfilled. There are so many things I want to do and so little I can accomplish," Radha asked, feeling exhilarated.

"The only thing standing between your desires and their fulfillment is you. Even in desiring you live a fragmented life. Your desires are weak. Today you desire this, tomorrow that; you sabotage yourself. It's like you put water on the stove to boil, and then after thirty seconds you put vegetable to cook instead. After another thirty seconds, you remember that you wanted to boil water, so you take the vegetable off and put the water back. Then you say there is something wrong with fire, the water is not boiling. Water has a boiling point. Once that is reached, it will boil, but you have to keep it on heat till then. You cannot blame water or fire, but your own impatience. You keep the fire inefficient by so many unnecessary thoughts and concepts. There should be some space in the mind for desires to manifest. You need to desire with the total presence of your being. *Fulfillment is not a favor but natural consequence of a desire.* When you clap, a sound comes; this is a fact, each and every time. You don't see how powerful you are, your tools of creation are: thoughts, words, and actions. If you knew that, you wouldn't waste time in scattered, unfocused, and random thoughts. Maybe you will get it, maybe not—this is your attitude. You live a repressed life believing that you are at the mercy of some invisible hand wishing for something magical to make things right. Even this repression is like burying a seed deep under snow-covered ground. The seed will sprout forth in the spring with rain and sun—that is when conducive environment is manifest."

Questions were bubbling inside Radha. She collected herself and asked, "Then how can I fulfill my desires sooner than later?"

"Desire fully and consciously—taste them, breathe them in your being. Always believe that whatever your desire, they are already a reality, which is, in fact, the reality."

In a flash Radha found herself walking along a path, somewhere in the woods leading to a huge lake, with the beggar walking along. It was a beautiful lake. *How she came there?* She looked at him with the incredulous expression of a child who had just found its ability to fly. Nevertheless, she was experiencing calm as she had never felt before.

He smiled and said humorously, "In deep layers of your heart you know it is true."

"Yes, multitudes of times I have done this and I know I have done this," she replied with trepidation. "I have created situations according to what I think and what I want to happen, and also what I fear. I have made things happen in my life. Since I don't think I am so powerful, I dismiss it as coincidence—or sometimes feel that my prayers have been answered."

"All of us have done this at some time or other," he responded.

"In truth, I feel scared. This power within me overwhelms me. It is too much of responsibility. So I deceive myself that it does not exist in me." Radha said.

"We have also created tragedies in our lives because we believe we deserve them. Too much happiness overwhelms us," he continued.

"Yes, and some tragedies are indeed welcome," Radha said.

"We feel victimized when lot of tragedies befall one after another. Why is it that happy people are becoming happier and sad people sadder? We deceive ourselves in believing that there is some outside force determining our fate. It is all inside, manifesting outside. The entire cosmos is within. Don't waste time looking outside, go inside; you will find everything there—wealth, joy, love, abundance."

Radha felt a burst of explosion within that left her startled. It was followed by a delicious warm feeling of joy.

The beggar said, "This is such a simple example. A parent always gives what a child wants. Even if the demand is not reasonable, a parent will still give in to the child if the child is relentless. What would you do if Abhi or Anya cries for a toy even though they have many toys?"

"I would reason with them."

"Does it work?"

"Not always. I distract them with the toys they already have."

"And does that work?"

"Sometimes—if that does not work, I say no. They just have to deal with it," Radha said.

"Then"

"Then..."

"That's not the end. If they still insist, throw a tantrum," the beggar pressed.

"Well, I give in and let them have what they want," Radha said in an impetuous tone.

"Even though you know it is not good for them."

"Do you think I am a bad parent?"

"I am just proving my point. When a child refuses to be distracted and remains relentless for what [2]he wants, the parent has to give in. It's not weakness, it is love. Then how can we think that the cosmos will not give us what we ask for when we are the children of the cosmos."

"But not always my desires get fulfilled," Radha asked doubtfully.

"That's because you get distracted. You lose focus and keep changing your mind. Be persistent and relentless, like the child who would

---

[2] A child can be a boy or girl. 'He' does not suggest that the child is a boy.

not stop till he gets what he wants. If your child gets lost, you won't eat, sleep, or do anything else till you find him. When you wish for something, desire it with your total presence; touch it with the breath of your soul. Your desires are not separate from the pure subjectivity of you. There is no power in this whole wide universe that can stop from manifesting your desires. Your own negativity and unbelief that you can get what you want hinders fulfillment. You desire, but you don't expect it to be fulfilled."

"Still, I have to work for it. I cannot get what I want just by thinking. This is unbelievable."

He smiled broadly and said, "The difference between wishful thinking and creative desire is enormous. Wishful thinking is not backed by anything, but behind every desire is an intention to act. Action always follows a desire. You will know more about it as you go along. Let me give you another example. If you wish to build a house, what steps will you take?"

"I will hire a contractor first," Radha replied.

"What else?"

"I will tell him what I want," she said.

"Like design specifications."

"Yes."

"What else?" The beggar asked.

"The contractor will buy appropriate materials and hire labor to construct the house," Radha said.

"What about affordability? You can have design specifications for a multimillion house, but if you have only a few hundred thousand, you cannot construct the house of your dreams, no matter what," the beggar said.

"Definitely affordability, that's a must," Radha said in agreement.

"You may want top of the line material, but without enough money, there is no way you can have the house of your wishes. The contractor will give you reasonable alternatives, like using cheaper materials. He will construct a house according to *your* budget and try to accommodate to *your* design specification. *You* will experience the house once completed, not the contractor."

"Sure."

"In the cosmic set up of things, the contractor is comparable to God, Process or Life; design specifications as wishes, longings and desires; affordability—your spiritual bank account—as actions, beliefs, and intense thoughts. God has no choice but to give you the life *you* wish for, according to *your* thoughts and actions. The contractor cannot build a house of his choice but what *you* want because he is working with *you*. He can advise but the ultimate choice is *yours*. *You* are the experiencer of the life *you* asked for. *You* gave the design specifications and God/Process/Life created that for *you*."

Radha stood by the lake, looking at its water sparkling in moonlight, perfect and calm. She wondered again how she came there, but realized it was one of those things she would never know.

"Consider your thoughts, words, and actions as your *spiritual bank account*. The more intense your thoughts and, therefore, your actions are, the more spiritual balance you have, positive or negative. Any thought which comes for the good of all, one that adds happiness—a thought of love, compassion, and kindness—increases your spiritual currency; any thought which comes as negativity for anyone, one that adds misery—a thought of envy, jealousy, hatred, and arrogance—deducts your spiritual currency. When you have more spiritual currency, you will enjoy a harmonious, enriching, and happy life—materially as well as spiritually, but if you have less spiritual currency, you will encounter many obstacles and lead a life of limitations."

"This is incredible," Radha said to herself.

"What is your favorite food?" he asked.

"Pizza"

"One day you have a desire to eat pizza. You go to a pizzeria and order a large pizza with extra toppings and everything. The shopkeeper asks for money. Pizza costs hundred rupees but you have only twenty. You ask him what you can get for twenty rupees. He hands you a slice with fewer toppings. You still have pizza, but in less quantity and quality. You going to pizzeria and ordering a pizza is *your* action, urged by *your* desire to eat one. *It is free will*. You order pizza, you get pizza. Just not exactly the way you want, but you cannot blame that on the shopkeeper. He makes and sells pizza only. You have to pay the price. This limitation, due to a shortage of currency, is your Karma."

A silence which a thousand words could not articulate ensued.

Radha sat down and waited, tears rolling down her cheeks. What was happening to her? True knowledge was embracing her, making love to her, and she was overwhelmed. She was ecstatic but also fearful, because it meant responsibility. It was no coincidence that such great knowledge was bestowed on her. She wanted it, longed for it for a long time, and had spent countless restless nights pondering the mystery of existence. Now it was coming, and it was coming in leaps and bounds. She had to breathe. *There is not a place where you would be taken that you had not wished for.*

"Are you even real? What if this is all a figment of my imagination?"

"I am here because you refuse to let me go. I have remained in your consciousness for a long time. Finally, with your inquisitiveness you have invited me to come and encounter you face to face."

They looked at each other, locked in silence. Radha drifted into a deep sleep. After some time—or a moment—she saw him looking at her. It seemed he didn't go anywhere but was watching the whole time she was sleeping, waiting for her to acknowledge his presence. She noticed a peculiar expression on his face as if he wanted to say more, as if he had some pain, some sadness—not his pain, but the world's pain—of not understanding the simplest thing there was to know.

Radha waited.

He began speaking carrying a powerful expression. Everything about him was powerful.

"The problem is not fulfillment of desires. There is an exact process for it, tools that need to be used whenever a wish, any longing has to be fulfilled: tools of thought and action, of belief and faith. The problem is the act of desiring itself."

"You lost me there. Everything in life is about dreams and living them?"

He smiled as a grown up smiles at a child and said, "Try to see through the illusion. You want this today you get it by appropriate thoughts and corresponding actions. Then a new desire arises, and you begin to work towards its fulfillment. This goes on endlessly. You have the free will to choose and act, but it traps you in its mysterious web. Your freedom is, in truth, your bondage. Try to grasp this fundamental truth—free will is the first step in destiny. If there is no free will, there is no destiny. You rise through power, and then this power becomes your nemesis."

"You have to explain more."

"You lose yourself in the ocean of wishes and desires and become imprisoned by your own free will, not someone else's. You are like a bird trapped in the cage made up of a strong wall of wishes and actions—your life is always an endeavor in some direction. You always have a need to be somebody, to reach somewhere. If you are the victim of life then you have created the victimization, not someone else. This bondage is your creation. You forget your real identity. You have infinite treasure in the middle, but you love to go around in circles thinking to have traveled a long distance, yet always remaining at the periphery. All you have to do is take one step inward, and you are at the destination. Even if you become the king of the world, you are still at the periphery.

Radha was too stunned to say anything.

"Life is the big drama which plays over and over from all angles," he said.

Radha looked at the beggar, and then she looked at the lake. She wondered, who or what was real—the beggar or the lake? What if she touched the beggar, would he disappear? She was still thinking when the beggar spoke again.

"Once a man lived who was well-versed in the secret of manifesting desires. He lived a good life because he would get whatever he wanted. It gave him immense thrill to know his own power. One day he thought what if a fire broke in the house, what would he do? That night, fire really engulfed the house with him in it. His thought power was so intense that just by thinking, he killed himself."

"Be careful what you wish for," Radha mumbled under her breath.

"The entire world is suffering from mistaken identities. You have a treasure and are begging for a nickel. You will understand and know in your heart your true identity when you are ready. Here, take this," he handed her a blue feather. "Keep it carefully. It will lead you to your destiny."

Radha has no further memory of what happened after she took the feather. She fell into a deep sleep.

≈ 4 ≈

Random Thoughts

"The important thing is not to stop questioning. Curiosity has its own rea-son for existing. One cannot help but be in awe when he contemplates the mysteries of eternity, of life, of the marvelous structure of reality. It is enough if one tries merely to comprehend a little of this mystery every day. Never lose a holy curiosity."—Albert Einstein

In the morning, Radha woke up startled. What happened? Did she actually meet the beggar, or was it a hallucination? If it was a dream, then what a lucid dream! She could still smell his presence on her breath.

She pondered on what the beggar had said about wishes and choic-es, desires and action, and about spiritual money. She lived a perfect life. She had a husband who doted on her, two wonderful children, great friends, and a successful career—she was a writer for children's books. She had reached a place everyone wanted to reach. But the charm that success and fame held had faded away. It had become an everyday phenomenon. There were times when everything felt worth-less and futile. She would wonder: *Is this it—now what?* Her soul was searching for something endless, waiting for something magical to happen. What? It didn't know. Her heart knew it existed. When she was trying to become someone, to achieve something, there was an expectation, fear of not attaining what she was aspiring to, a thrill of going somewhere. Now when she was there, it didn't feel that good. It seemed something was missing.

It was on those days she wondered what would happen if one achieved everything one had ever wished for: It would be the most unfortunate thing that could happen. It meant that it was the end; there would be nothing more to do, no dreams to go after, no aspirations to work for. People live—their whole lives—doing what suits their fancy, have family and careers, bask in self glory for some time feeling all important and powerful, always fearing losing it all. Even then, eventually, everyone dies. So many generations took birth before me, lived their lives, and died. There was no beginning and no end to the cycle of life and death. Everyone was keeping themselves busy with thoughts and activities of self pursuit, so that there was no space in the minds to think about what they were doing—wishing for something miraculous to happen. After all material prosperity will keep all of us happy. But will it satisfy us...our hunger for something great, greater than ourselves.

Later that day, Radha stood at the window watching the sun set beyond the lush green mountains. The sky had turned various colors of orange and purple. It was a stunning sight. It took her breath away. She lived at the top of a hill which gave her a treetop view of the woods. It always filled her with wonder when she looked at the immensity of creation from there. Dusk turned into night, and she stood there without moving, lost in her thoughts. Finally, she looked up. A full moon adorned the sky. Under the same moon, she thought, Gautama Buddha roamed the world, Krishna advised Arjuna, mystics lost themselves in divine ecstasy, Isaac Newton discovered gravity, and Albert Einstein pondered upon the mysteries of the universe. It was the same moon her ancestors saw every night, day after day for ages. She was mesmerized by the timelessness of the moon and space itself, keeping her in a safe cocoon.

She was still bewildered at the advent of the beggar in her dreams. Was he a reality in some dimension? If her unconscious mind was creating him, how did she know the answers to her own questions? If the beggar was answering, then he was not part of her mind. She remembered his face was gleaming in the moonlight. There was a full moon in real life too. So it was not a dream, and it was not waking life. It was something else, some dimension in the middle or beyond.

Little did she know that she was walking on a razor's edge. Unknowingly, through her intense desire to know the purpose of life and her real identity in relation to the world, she had set off a chain of events that would lead her to the deepest corners and, eventually, put her at the edge of the mind. From there she had to take the giant leap of faith in the unknown, drowning herself in the ocean of consciousness unknown to human mind. She never expected answers would come from such mysterious source and in such a manner.

The next day, Radha was totally exhausted by the activities of the day. As day turned into dusk, she stood in front of a huge mirror hanging on the wall. It was an antique brass mirror she inherited from her grandfather. It must have been hundred years old. Whenever she wanted to clarify her thoughts, she'd look at her reflection in the mirror and ponder.

Were they living in a real world or was it an illusion, she wondered. She stared at her reflection. After a while she began to feel something infinite—something grand and glorious—behind those eyes, looking back. It was the same greatness she saw whenever she looked at other's eyes—human or animal. Somehow, she knew it was one and the same principle which resided in her and everyone else. What was it? She felt a need to get to this phenomenon. Sometimes it was so close she could touch it and sometimes so far off she could hardly feel it, but it was always giving her power, making her glorious.

Radha felt her heartbeat quicken as she saw a blue feather protruding from under the pillow. She examined the mysterious feather. It was real, not fancy of her mind. During the past two days she had shrugged off the beggar dream as simply a dream. Now she was not sure. She had to get her thoughts in order and be prepared if the beggar reappeared in her dream. She felt like an alien in an alien world where everyone was in deep slumber and did not want to wake up.

To distract herself from her restless thoughts, Radha opened the television. A gentleman was giving a speech. Suddenly he looked straight in her eyes and said: *We all are living in a dream. We are playing a*

game and have forgotten all about it. Everything in life has be-
come real to us but, in reality, it is just an illusion.

Radha jumped to her feet. She rubbed her eyes. Had she heard cor-
rectly? What was happening? Was she losing her mind? Whoever was
working behind the conspiracy was determined to give her a heart attack. Just yesterday she was leading a regular life and in one day she
was becoming immersed in a mysterious world full of wonder. As she
slept that night, the strangest feeling came over her. She felt like Alice
in Wonderland.

She was frightened and excited at the same time.

The next day, she went for her usual morning walk at 5 am. It was
something she looked forward to. Fresh dew drops on the leaves, birds
just beginning to wake up—extraordinary events taking place every
day, from tiny blades of grass to the immense sky. Life burst forth
every morning filling her with energy.

She looked at a huge oak tree and though: The magnificent expanse
of a tree is hidden in such a little seed. What is inside a seed as to make
this kind of astounding evolution into a tree, and so effortlessly and
naturally! There is magic all around us. Seeds grow into trees, days
turn into nights, caterpillars transform into butterflies. What could be
more magical and elegant than nature at its work.

There is nothing new that we, as humans, have created which is not
already there. We have just uncovered the principles hidden in nature
and used them for our purpose. We have learned from the root system
of trees to build buildings, from birds' the principles of aerodynamics,
from spider webs the strength of geometric patterns. We cannot create.
To create means to make something out of nothing. We can only un-
cover and unveil—like a sculpture from a heap of clay, a statue from a
rock, a form from the formless. The entire universe is a vast womb of
potential. Everything imaginable can be manifested from this infinite
pool of consciousness. In that sense, we have uncovered this marvelous
world around us.

Even the human mind is not random. There is a whole structure to
it, such great mystery and perfection in design. There might be lots of
other unknown forces and things which exist now. Just because science

has not yet discovered them does not mean they do not exist. I find myself encompassed by a big wide universe. There is nothing I can say is mine and everything in it is mine. The immense space upholds me, sustains me, and loves me; otherwise, I would have been crushed to pieces the moment I was born. The fact that I am living is a wonder in itself. A phenomenon makes me born into this world, in this body. I might as well have not been born. A thing profound is working in the background which is all-compassionate and loving. It is filled with love and joy, and holds me in its womb like a mother holds a baby.

Radha was amazed by the thoughts that came to her whenever she was alone.

That night, Radha was in good spirits. She was humming and cooking dinner when Suraj returned home.

"Isn't it great to be alive?" Radha kissed Suraj.

Suraj was surprised at her sudden display of affection. It wasn't something she usually did. He was happy that she was happy. Suraj knew something was bothering her.

"Yes, it is great to be alive and kicking," Suraj said.

"What'd you think if one day you realize you are living in a dream and nothing is real?" Radha asked.

Suraj had got used to her strange questions. It was one of the reasons he loved her more. Usually people have gotten used to the world and have lost their sense of wonder. He enjoyed philosophical conversations with Radha. It gave him something to think about and kept the balance in their life. But sometimes her questions scared him. It was one of those questions.

"I wonder why everybody is busy acquiring things, status, and wealth. Nobody seems to be interested in looking at what make them go round. Who are they? Mysterious creatures inhabiting Earth with no memory of who or what they were, as if they magically appeared here one day and started living in such self-forgetfulness that even the question as to their existence does not arise in their minds?"

"I have married a mysterious creature from outer space," Suraj laughed.

"Don't you see how quickly everything in life becomes a habit, both pleasure and sorrow, love and fear. Everyday mundane things first offer boredom, and then given some time become delight. They begin to give feeling of security and habits become means of escape," Radha continued.

"Am I a habit or security?" There was a worried look on Suraj's face. He could not deny the truth in her words. Over time, everyday things had become the source of security for him—his job, house, friends, Radha, and even Abhi and Anya. He smiled nervously. Radha smiled back.

That was the last thing they talked about that night before retiring to the couch, watching their favorite shows. It was the time they spend together as a family, feeling all comfortable and cozy in each other's presence.

That night, when Radha slept she took the blue feather in her hand and woke up to find herself under a huge Banyan tree. There was a big hollow space at the bottom of the trunk. It seemed sacred. She looked inside. Immense peace was radiating in all directions. She looked around. It was the same woods she visited every morning. She even recognized the path leading up to her house

"The monk is waiting for you," a blue jay bird said.

In one day Radha had learned not to be surprised to hear a bird talking human language. Anything can happen in a dream, if it is a dream.

She felt a pair of eyes watching her. She had never seen anything like them. They shone with the brilliance of the sun. It took everything in her to stay calm. And the face it belonged to. It had the soothing calmness of the moon. A white robe adorned his body. He was a young monk with perfectly calm expression on his face. He looked at her with an unknown compassion.

"What do I have to do to reach somewhere?" she asked quickly, afraid he might vanish in the corners of dream space. She had thought all day about what she would ask.

"Where do you want to reach?" the monk asked.

"I don't know. I only know I want to reach somewhere, achieve something where I feel I have accomplished something, done something with my life."

"Why do you want to accomplish something?" he asked pleasantly.

"To feel happy and peaceful, I guess." She was awed at her response. She had never pondered on *why* she wanted to accomplish something.

"You are already there where you want to reach," he said with authority.

"But I don't feel I am already there."

"That's because you are sleeping. You don't have to do anything even to wake up. Once the course of sleep is done, you'll wake up on your own. No effort is needed. Do you see seeds making any effort to grow? They just grow effortlessly. Whatever is needed to make them survive is already provided: sun, water, and earth. Look at nature. Look at harmony of things; do you see any effort anywhere, any struggle whatsoever? Do you see majestic birds making an effort to fly, butterflies trying to be beautiful or water trying to flow? This tremendous universe is running spontaneously without any orders, without any commandments. Life is effortless. You have made it a struggle with your pursuit to become something or someone; always trying to become, never a being," he said simply.

Radha saw a number of different bugs crawling on the ground and heard many different sounds. She was mesmerized to see so much life in and around one tree. A whole another universe existed in a single tree.

"When you fly from one city to another, the airplane would take you there. You unnecessary make an effort by worrying, 'will it reach its destination, what I need to do to reach safely.' You are neither the pilot of the plane nor the technician that you can be aware of any problem with its running or maintenance. You cannot fix what you are not aware of or of what you have no understanding. You can trust the capability of the flight crew. There is a science behind the working of an airplane. Various processes are already set and streamlined to have its smooth running. Your stress and planning is not going to increase the speed or slow it down. Yes, it might make your journey stressful, and you can cause stress to fellow passengers, for which you cannot blame anyone except yourself. All you need to do is sit and enjoy the journey," he further explained.

Radha stared at him with inexplicable wonder.

"Some mist is covering your mind, hindering you to see that you have already accomplished what you want to accomplish. All you have to do is enjoy the moment. Life is a celebration." He was looking at her intensely, with compassion all around his being.

Radha felt loved and cared for by the entire cosmos.

"But I have to make an effort. How will I achieve anything if I don't work for it? That would mean quitting. After all what is the purpose of life?" Radha needed more time to grasp the meaning.

"Life means joy. It signifies nothing. You give meaning to it with your thoughts and opinions, and then actions. You have a blank slate and can create whatever you want, infinite possibilities for a lifetime. But first you have to let go of all conditioning, all the fictions and stories your mind has created around you. *Create*. Life is meant to create. But create for the pure joy of creation. Create out of love, and love every moment of it. Do not make your life a struggle by identifying with it." He looked like a teacher giving a lecture in college.

"If you live in Delhi and go to Mumbai for work, you come back to Delhi after finishing your work. That is the purpose of life. You come back home from where you started. The meaning is the meaning you create with your thoughts, beliefs and choices, the work you assign yourself in Mumbai. Your choice becomes the cause for the next effect (situation, event, or person) in life, and that effect will become the next cause depending on how you choose to act on it. If it is a good thing or bad is again depended on how you react to it, with joy or with sorrow. Cause and effect—it works *with* you, not *for* you. Destiny is nothing but free will working through you. It is a matter of choice, not of chance."

Radha stood motionless, filled with wonder.

"Another way to look at it, there are twenty-six letters in English alphabet. Whether it is a sleazy fiction of romance and crime, or timeless classic of Shakespeare, a book is an arrangement of twenty-six different letters only. But see how different arrangements make such enormous difference in books? How you arrange your life is entirely up to you.

Alphabets do not show any partiality or preference to one person over another. How you use them is based on your choice. Like a writer, you have to write it—life and its meaning; like an artist you have to carve it. The purpose of your life is not sitting somewhere to be discovered, but it exists as a desire in your heart."

Radha was blissfully aware of his soothing voice showering eternal wisdom.

"In reality, life is just a journey from home to back home. Always remember, it is a game started for creation, expression and experience. We are players and all players are important. No one is superior or inferior to another. All are the same. Problems arise when we become identified with our games and think that they are the reality and experience emotions of losing and winning associated with it," he further explained.

"Yes, I heard about life being a game before. Did you send the television person?"

"May be you invited him," he said mysteriously.

"May be, I invited you too."

"May be you did."

"What's your name?"

"What's in a name?" He said before going through the path leading to Radha's house.

Radha looked at the path and picked up a dead leaf lying on the ground. She wondered: would she reach her home if she followed the monk. She couldn't resist and began to follow him, but as soon as the house began to appear before her, she lost consciousness.

≈ 5 ≈

The Mystery Deepens

"The most beautiful experience we can have is the mysterious." — Albert Einstein

Radha woke up with a start. She looked at the watch. It was only three in the morning, but she was wide awake. Then, she remembered everything. Unable to sleep, she went in the kitchen to pour herself a glass of warm milk. As the milk was warming, she went to stand by the window overlooking the backyard. She was startled to see the same monk in the white robe standing in the backyard, looking straight at her. When he was sure her attention was caught, he waved her good-bye.

Radha rushed to the door leading to the backyard, her heart pounding fast. She was a little too late. The monk was nowhere in sight. Something else caught her attention. It was a blue feather similar to the one the beggar had given her, on the exact spot where the monk was standing. She was sure the feather wasn't there earlier.

So it hadn't been a dream after all. Could she have really seen the monk from her dream? How could she see someone in real life who existed in a dream? Was it possible that the distance between the real and dreaming world was not so wide after all? Did both dimensions meet somewhere? She was too exhausted to think. Yet sleep was miles away. Her mind was full of questions, and there was no one to turn to. She could not involve Suraj. She knew she had been transported to a different realm. How and why—that she had to find out. She was sure the road to solving the mystery lay in the mystery itself. It led inwards. She had to let the mysterious envelope her totally, before she could begin to understand it.

When Radha woke up the next morning the sun was already up in the sky. Suraj had left for work, and the twins were fed and playing in their room. She decided to take a detour from her usual routine of working from home—she was rewriting and perfecting the script for a new book she was presently working on. Before leaving that day, she made sure the twins were with their nanny. She picked up the mysterious feathers, got in her car, and drove. She tried to remember what the monk had said.

Everything is effortless. The thought made her feel good.

She drove east for an hour going through forest-covered foothills. The landscape was rich in color and blindingly beautiful. Cypress and oak trees marked the sides of the road. She was stuck by the incredible wonder of nature, so mesmerized by the stunning beauty spread before her that no thought crossed her mind for some time. She forgot who or where she was, and was slightly aware of a delight filling her slowly from the bottom to the top. She drove, rest of the way, relishing every moment.

She stopped in front of a big structure that looked like an Ashram. Radha noticed nothing had changed since she was there a few months earlier. The grounds were nicely kept. The gravel walkways were edged with bushes, and the grass was recently mowed. The view of the mountains from there was staggering. She recognized Guruji sitting cross legged on the marble floor in the main hall. As she looked at him, he opened his eyes and looked straight at her as if he knew she was watching him. He smiled and motioned her to walk up.

He was a man of medium height of about fifty years of age. His face had a unique glow seen in spiritual people after they had done years of intellectual as well as spiritual practices. He was a powerful man in the spiritual community. Everyone loved and respected him and called him Guruji, the master. He carried immense presence around himself and was always surrounded by love and laughter. Radha felt she was at the right place.

"How is your breathing practice going?" He asked.

"Fine, but I am here for a different reason," Radha answered.

"People experience different things in the beginning as they start doing breathing techniques. Do not be bothered by them. It shows you are advancing. Certain things are getting adjusted in your system. It also shows that you are a diligent student." He had an infectious smile.

Radha smiled back, showed him blue feathers, and told him about her encounter with the beggar and the monk.

Guruji did not say anything. She was unable to read the expression on his face. After some silence, he finally said in a slow voice, almost whispering, "We have become so immersed in playing the game of life that we have started to believe in its reality."

"What is the obsession with game? Why does everyone keep saying that I am playing a game? Why do I choose to play a game in the first place, and why can't I stop playing if I want?"

"Be grateful for the game. It is the answer to your prayers. If you stop playing, you'd stop creating, expressing and experiencing. There is nothing else to do," he said in a finale.

"I don't understand." She crossed her arms with a sigh of frustration.

He looked at her with eyes deep with an unknown understanding, "There is a mystery enveloping this whole creation. Why are you worried about the purpose of all this? Critical word is—*enjoy*. You began this game of life for fun and, somehow, began to identify with it. With identification comes misery."

He was saying the same thing the monk in her dream had said. Were they both connected in some way, she wondered.

"Life is a stage. You are an actor enacting your part according to the script you have. You have to remember you are the actor of your own story as well as the director, producer, and also the scriptwriter, even the camera and the projector. You are limited by your nature and belief system, your thoughts and perception; this is bondage. You have a choice to become aware of your thoughts and actions. Then you would be able to direct your life the way you want. Life would no longer be the bondage but a creative tool to create your own destiny," he said.

"I think I am beginning to understand," Radha said.

"The dimension you experience now was put there because you asked for it. There are sacred dimensions to this world untouched by any word or action, pure and divine. Your soul yearns for it. What you do with it is entirely up to you. The only qualification required is an urge to know, a desire to remember." He got up, indicating the meeting was over. Then, suddenly, as if remembering something, he said, "Sometimes repetition is necessary to understand. Always remember, Eternity and Infinity resides in the deepest recess of your heart. It can be experienced only in the present moment. Your own heart harbors the greatest secret of the entire creation."

Radha was thrown in the space of eternity. She remembered nothing; she forgot nothing. Suspended in time, she felt her whole life in a moment. She realized it was the present moment that existed and nothing else. To be in the present moment is to plunge into eternity.

She had visited the sanctuary six months back. It was a famous place within the spiritual circle. A group of monks lived there leading spiritual life. People would come and listen to them as they gave discourses on Creation and its divine mystery. Sheila, her friend, was very impressed with the talks given and had asked Radha to go there at least once. When she went to the retreat for the first time Radha heard Guru-ji say in his discourse: 'You are your own cause and your own effect. You are the unknown force in the universe. You are in all space and time. The only responsibility you have is to know yourself.'

She had stood there, frozen, for a long time.

They—the monks—didn't belong to any religion and preached that one should believe in experience rather than what was told through generations and generations of conditioning. They taught meditation, day in day out, believing that to be the path to experience the ultimate reality rather than what was taught by the religious community. They didn't say God existed or not existed. They urged people to explore to the very end till they remember and experience and arrive. They asked the devotees to doubt everything. The proof of an ice cream is eating it, one doesn't believe in it, they said. The question of belief does not arise, because it exists, and one tastes and experiences. Knowing needs no belief. Why should God be otherwise? A true religion does not require faith; a true religion requires experience.

Radha remembered Guruji had glanced at the people sitting in the hall as if they were him, and with a loving voice he had said: 'Know yourself because by knowing yourself you can know everything else, the infinite, and the eternal. There is no other way. It is the greatest discovery and the only pilgrimage you are required to take.'

Radha had asked, still in dazed state, after the lecture was finished, 'How can I know myself? I can know this world. I can go to the moon and space. There is enough technological advancement for humankind to do all these things, but how do I know myself?'

'The thing which cannot be known has to be transcended, because it happens to be the self. Through stilling your mind you can know and transcend yourself. Your mind is hindering you from reaching yourself. It is filled with stories, ideas and concepts, and it creates such a thick veil that cannot be penetrated, except by right knowledge and right perception. When the mind becomes silent, true knowledge comes. Magic word is *Observation*. Be a scientist: observe, dissect, analyze, and finally dissolve what is called the mind. Observe every wisp of thought, every reaction—inside and out. Be aware of all impulses, memories, thoughts, and imagination, but see them as visitors— friendly forces which pay you a visit now and then. Treat them as you would treat other visitors to your house. Receive them with pomp and joy, but do not identify with them. Make your mind a lab. The only thing you can trust is yourself. The same mind can, then, be used for upliftment. Make your life an exploration, a pilgrimage of the mind and spirit. When you observe and go deeper into yourself, you will find a tremendous reality—the point of the Big Bang, the beginning of Creation. You can have its direct perception because it is not located at some point in space and time. It is always here and now.' He had given the timeless answer.

Unable to walk, Radha needed to sit down and collect herself. She looked around. The place was bursting with people. They had come from different places to do the meditation course. Despite the presence of so many people, the place was surrounded with peace and calm.

Away from the hubbub of city, it was adorned with natural beauty. Different plants with rainbow of colors marked the gardens. Butterflies were everywhere. She found an empty spot on a bench and sat down.

She thought of all the things leading her to this moment. It was only six months earlier she lived a perfectly normal life. But something was missing. There was always something she failed to grasp. During the day she was busy with family and work, but in the nights strange thoughts came to torment her. Those were not thoughts for intellectual discussion; she felt the urgency, restlessness, and torment of them as if they were people following her everywhere, mocking her ignorance. The thoughts would come from inside her, from deep somewhere whose existence she was not aware of. Sometimes they would come in flashes, and for a moment she'd become aware of something of her own, intimate and close, and then they would be gone. She wondered what they were—part of her intellect or something above the intellect.

She had felt an impulse to write her thoughts. So, in nights, when everyone was asleep she would write. Once she began, thoughts would gush forth as if waiting for the door to open. So many times she got scared from what came outside. Consciously she didn't remember thinking like that. But in the stillness of night they would come to shake the very foundation of the mind she was standing on.

Now standing amongst the splendor of garden sanctuary, Radha didn't feel like going back home. Weather was pleasant and the view stunning. She thought: I stare at my eyes reflected in the mirror. I keep looking for some time. I see a different person there, a grand presence. My mind puzzles me. I feel whole eternity there. Why couldn't I look in my own eyes and not feel overwhelmed? I am finite. I have a body. I exist for some time and die, just like everybody else. I am limited, confronted by the universe all around. Nature can crush me out of existence at a moment's notice. There is something called thirst over which I have no control. I feel cold, and I feel hungry. I am forced to eat; otherwise, I will die of starvation. I have no choice. I am mesmerized by the workings of nature. It has tremendous power over me. Every action of the body and mind is forced out of me. My thoughts are not mine either. They are coming from somewhere, from beyond the edge of the mind. I am a slave to this force.

Yet as soon as I look in my eyes, I see myself surrounded by something greater than myself, a thing grand and infinite. I try to grasp it. I have come to a point where my experience contradicts which I have understood in the realm of reason. My intellect has brought me here. It can only take me as far as its boundaries. It is a contradiction which I cannot grasp. Everything in life is so vast that intellect is nothing compared to it. Life refuses to be bound by the laws of intellect. I take my life as finite, but as soon as I begin to analyze it with my thoughts and experiences, there is no end to their (life and its experiences) possibilities and powers. Soon they elude my knowledge and plunge into the abyss of infinite. My world becomes infinite. There is something in me having a larger dimension than my present personality, transcending me. What or who is this? The question puzzles me even more. Who am I? It is the only question I have to find answer to. 'I, myself' is the greatest mystery of the universe.

I find myself thinking about it all the time. It exists. It has to exist, otherwise it cannot beckon me, summon me with such an intensity. My mind cannot be tormented by something imaginary. This wholeness has to exist as a complete answer to my incomplete endeavor.

It was after her first visit to the Ashram, Radha had enrolled herself in the meditation course. Over the course of four days various breathing techniques were taught to bring the mind to the present moment. If she could practice every day, it would do wonders for her, so she was told. Like a diligent student, she practiced for few days, and then the haze started to lift away. The mist which was always clouding her intellect began to clear. As she started doing conscious breathing, Radha began to be aware of her higher self. After a while she felt exhilarated, her body was filled with a well being.

Later she wrote: This is intimate, my breath, staying with me all the time. Nothing else is so close and nobody so near. My breath is coming from me, but belonging to some mysterious unending source. It sustains me through everything. Who or what has attuned me to breathe, without an effort on my part? Is breath God? I feel welcomed.

Breathe in and breathe out. As I breathe in and out I am becoming aware of a presence in my breath. I come to an astounding realization that there is someone else in me too. Someone or something is hiding behind the breath. There is a mystery. I feel close to this person or entity. Gradually, understanding dawns on me that this thing—so intimate—is not something external but my own higher dimension. It is not just me but the whole universe with its various creative and experiencing powers! When I am breathing, the universe in its totality is breathing through me! Each and every part of the cosmos—space enveloping and pervading everything—is breathing through me, with me! I have become the cosmos! Pleasure fills me and I dance in various raptures of joy.

My heart delights in this endless captivating mystery. It is the gateway to a different world, the real world. It is as close as I am to myself yet slips away as soon as I begin to think, to analyze, and to solve the mystery. Thoughts, too hard to capture, tame me, and I lose myself in the scattered activities of the mind. The pride I have in my intellect is gone in a moment.

I am becoming aware of a phenomenon, higher than me, bestowing knowledge on me. Even the pride in knowledge that I have is not mine but this higher entity's, which has been controlling me, my senses and perception all the time. It is more like loving me in the most affectionate and compassionate way. The impact it has on my perception is profound. All thoughts vanish and a feeling of goodness fills every part of my body. My entire being is filled with goodness like a pitcher is filled with water. Such a good feeling that nothing else matters; all that matters is the present moment where I belong. There is no place on this earth where I would rather belong than the present moment. The present moment is eternity. The rest is unreal.

I feel touched by the divine. I have never felt so close to existence. The Divine is sitting in the same room, looking at me, smiling, making friends, and playing with me compassionately. I can feel the presence everywhere. It is intoxicating, mesmerizing, blissful, and complete. Pleasure and pain cannot touch the presence of divine. It does not depend on anything. Nothing can find or hold *It*. It is *a thing in itself* and can only be experienced in the present moment, at the deepest core of my being. Oh, what joy! The whole universe bows down to *It*. The sun, the moon, and the countless galaxies are dependent on *It*. It exists beyond this world yet *It* exists within my heart. It is the point of the Big Bang. My mind cannot think like that. My mind does not know what to think of. It is an experience where I melt into incomparable joy without a beginning and an end. So much peace, such calm, endless joy descends… and then thoughts come back and capture me. I start thinking. I do not want to think. I want the feeling of the divine to persist little longer, but my mind refuses to obey me. I am amazed at the mind's power over me.

Radha's world changed after that. She was getting more and more engulfed in the mystery and felt cherished by it. The sun was starting to set. She could not stay longer. She had to pick the twins, she remembered. So many thoughts were starting to gather in her mind. As she drove back, she reflected about what the monk in the dream had said: Life is effortless. We are unnecessarily making it a struggle due to the filter of our minds. The divine is right in front of us and we choose not to look. Why we don't look at it this way? Why do we ignore this possibility? We have become so numb from everyday mundane things, from our way of thinking that everything is supposed to be a struggle. It is hard to see that something so beautiful and elegant, something so enigmatic, something so incomprehensible can be so simple. We have to struggle more, shed more tears, more tragedies, more fears, and more failures before we begin to understand the divine cosmic energy and its play; accept and embrace it. The Truth—holy—is not going anywhere. It has always been with us through the beginning of creation and loved us through thick and thin. We all have been perfect for *It* no matter what we did. It does not judge us. It does not expect anything from us. It just simply is and does what *It* does best—love us. It is only when we begin to acknowledge *It*, *It* embraces us.

Nobody talks about the phenomena of Reality. Going after career, success, wealth has become more important. We don't apply our tools in finding answers to the eternal questions. We would rather make nuclear weapons and fight to establish control over others. Once we establish control over the world we won't become powerful but, in-

stead, would become more fearful of losing control. Why not try to establish control over ourselves first. Observe how we behave, what mo-
tivates us. Observe our minute to minute thoughts, feelings, and actions. We are the most mysterious creatures. Instead of finding ourselves, we are going after the objects outside. They are not going anywhere. We don't talk about these things. We don't understand these
things and, therefore, ignore them. Finding material success is so much
easier.

She was still deeply lost in her thoughts when she reached home. It
was late in night. Suraj and kids were fast asleep.

≈ **6** ≈

The Aha Moment

"Life is illusionary like images on still water. We take it as real but, it is just images on water. As you throw a pebble in still water you become aware that you are staring at the image. When we keep looking at still water on a lake, reflections on it seem real, but they are reflections only."

The next day, Radha woke up late. The sun was out in full glory, naked and proud, filling every corner of the sky with its glorious splendor. Abhi and Anya came yawning and slept besides her. She looked at them. They were so innocent and beautiful.

She wondered: What did I do to deserve such beautiful gifts from heaven? Why did they love me so much? I am grateful to the universe for giving me the experience of motherhood and bringing me closer to love. Through the love of mother and child I can have the glimpse of higher love—love of that magnificent all pervading intelligence. At the same time this love is my chain. Would I have loved Abhi and Anya with the same intensity and feeling if they were not my children? Maybe they were my neighbors' children. My friends have kids. I don't love them the way I love my kids. I imagine Anya as someone else's daughter and just by switching, my feeling for her changes. Now she is a friend's daughter. She is good but mine is better. Do I really love my kids or it is 'my' that I love—because they are my kids. I love myself and everything that belongs to me.

Suddenly its implication hit her, and she was struck with surprise and awe. She remembered when she was young— maybe five or six years old—she had always wondered why her parents loved her so much, because she was her or because she was their child? What if she was not their child but somebody else's? Would she have loved them if they were not her parents? She always considered their love selfish, because they loved her for not what she was but because she was their child. She considered herself selfish too, because she could not love her parents without the condition of the relationship—of parent-child. Radha had not thought about it in a long time and now it was all coming back to her.

She thought: It is in plain sight, but I choose not to look. Look at the cleverness of mind, so quick in discarding what it does not want to accept! I don't love anybody except myself. In my eyes I am the most important person, and everybody else is secondary. Such is the power of ego. I, as a human, have invaded space; I have gone to the moon, but I am still not able to decipher what and who I am. I believe in my separate story and seek to find lasting happiness in the relationships of spouse, children, colleagues, and friends. I have a need to feel loved, to belong. I escape and live in the past or future rather than understand and live in the present. I am not interested in others. As long as others agree with me I am satisfied, not a moment more.

Does love really exist, or is it some word that I have discovered to satisfy my mind? But how do I, then, explain countless moments when I feel the depths of love in my being. In these moments I do not even remember that I exist. These moments don't last; nevertheless, they exist—when breathtaking beauty render me speechless, when I look into a child's eyes, when I look at the sky, when butterflies flutter, when flowers bloom, when season's change, when the wind blows, when it rains. The list is endless and experiences short. These experiences give me a glimpse of the wonderful world of love and beauty, without any conditions, profound and deep.

I do not see this world of glory, so immersed I am in my ambitions, fears, memories, and in pursuit of future. How foolish I am. I am standing in the ocean and thirsty for water. Love exists. It has to exist. It is a cosmic phenomenon. It is not a thing to be cultivated or developed. It is spontaneous. It is much bigger than me. I have felt its immense force multitude of times, and it has scared me since I cannot possess it.

That evening, returning from work, as Radha was corning the curve leading to the house, she was met by her neighbor of five years, Anita. She was delighted to see her. With time, they got busy with their lives and just didn't have the time to catch up anymore. Though they didn't talk about it, they both knew of a strong invisible bond between them, a bond of sharing, caring, and an unknown connection which seemed to hold everything together, integrating the whole universe. She was tempted to tell Anita about her recent adventures in other dimension but decided against it. She felt overwhelmed to look in her eyes. There was a magnetic quality to them pulling her in. She was sure it wasn't there before. Was Anita also part of the plan? She wondered.

Abhi and Anya were playing in the backyard. Radha hurried to start dinner. She was beginning to feel the start of a mild headache. As body gets used to a pattern and any day the pattern is broken, it reacts in some way. She didn't have her evening tea, she realized. It was a ritual she was following for fifteen years. Her body was used to it. She relished every sip of tea, first in her mouth, and then in her being. She put the tea kettle on stove.

For some reason the trip to the Ashram the day before had invigorated her. There was something, she couldn't pinpoint, happening at the background of her existence, something extraordinary. She always wondered if something greater than humanity existed, a substratum of existence. She was always looking for it, longing for it. Now she knew it existed, and it existed very near and close, so near that she could touch it and so elusive that she failed to fathom it. There was a veil she hit every time she tried to touch it. It was pure bliss and joy; at the same time, it offered so much misery.

She was tucking the twins for the night when Suraj returned. They ate dinner talking about the events of the day. He was in good spirits. He had returned from a two day business trip from Mumbai. It had turned out better than he expected. She told him about her day at work and her trip to the ashram the previous day.

Suraj looked at her in wonder. Sometimes he thought he lived with a stranger. Radha had charmed him the first time they had met at her cousin's house, eleven and a half years ago. They dated for a year before getting married. He thought he knew her well, but there were days like the present one when he was not sure. They had been together for so many years, and her strange disposition has stopped bothering him. He loved her too much, but sometimes he got worried. She was an accomplished woman with great books to her credit, most often fantasy for children. She conducted herself well in social gatherings and could be very charming. But then she would go into her shell, thinking and talking about strange things like she did the other day about everything not being real. Having a thoughtful mind was a good quality, but it had nothing to do with everyday reality. Success, hunger, heat, and cold were real issues to human existence.

Radha looked at him. Her husband was not her husband. Her children were not her children. She loved her husband and children but there were moments when they were strangers to her, and she wanted to escape, just disappear into nothingness. She looked at her house, recognized it, but stood apart from it as if it belonged to a stranger. She saw herself as if she were looking at someone else. She felt her presence; observed it as if it was separate from her. She did not belong at any one place, but that she was everywhere and observed everything with wonder. She could not negate the fact that she loved her life but felt guilty that at the end of the day she was glad that it had come to an end, and she could coil back into her thoughts. She'd feel empty as if whatever was supposed to be done was done and there was nothing more to do. Everything which had ever belonged to her was taken away. The loss of possessions brought relief too. Since she had nothing which belonged to her, she no longer had to protect anything and no longer had to fear losing it. *She had become free.*

She looked at the neighbor's houses and thought: All of us have lives, families, and careers. We all have our own desires and fears, tragedies and triumphs. We are friends, spouses, parents, inventors, workers. But we are not just a friend, parent or spouse. These are included in us. We are much more than these relationships. Who are we—the biggest enigma and the greatest mystery of all times.

Everyone is connected with each other by a powerful, invisible force. I don't know what it is, but it is immense and beautiful. Just as all the fingers are connected to the palm; similarly, everyone is connected to this invisible force. What is it which connects me to the whole universe? I can feel it... something strong, and yet fragile. There is this grandness about the whole thing—a power without a direction or cause which is all sublime, like beauty which cannot be seen but felt. I try to capture it, but it is elusive. Is it God?

≈ 7 ≈

The Illusion of Joy and Sorrow

"The deeper the sorrow carves into your being, the more joy you can contain. When you are joyous, look deep into your heart and you shall find it is only that which has given you sorrow that is giving you joy. When you are sorrowful look again in your heart, and you shall see that in truth you are weeping for that which has been your delight." —Khalil Gibran

Radha could not take her mind of the feathers. She took them out and examined them one more time. Extraordinary events were taking place beyond her control. Usually she would prefer to be in control, but this time it was different. She was enjoying the feeling of abandon—like being on a roller coaster ride. Once the ride was on, she just had to sit back and trust whatever was out there and enjoy the adventure.

Her headache from the previous day had increased. Finally, she gave in and took painkillers. After some time it started to go—and what a relief! She experienced great joy. It was still there but receding somewhere in the mind and becoming a memory. How great was the state of well-being. She felt grateful for the pain to go away and pleasure to set in.

And then she began to realize like a revelation, even though she had heard it so many times—that the high state was always there. She did not have headaches all the time. Her natural state was well-being and health. But to be aware of her natural state, she has to first come down to experience a lower state. If she didn't have pain she wouldn't know pleasure. Pleasure and pain did not have any independent existence. They don't exist...!

She began to feel drowsy because of the medication. No sooner had she closed her eyes, she saw fishes swimming. It wasn't a dream. Blue, orange, golden, red—rainbow of colors of fishes—they were passing through beautiful corals under sea, swimming in her, through her. One came towards her. As soon as it reached her in the space of her mind, it merged with her. She was the boundary. The sea existed in her! Wherever she was, the place seemed to contain an unfathomable secret. The sea appeared to grow in size in whatever direction she took. It was endless. She was dumbfounded to realize that she had become one with that which existed in the space inside the water, so much so that her own body had ceased to exist; she had become the sea, spread everywhere, flowing joyously.

Radha opened her eyes in amazement. After a moment she closed them again. This time she heard a roar through water. It was a faint rumbling which grew louder and louder as she moved. Suddenly she came to the surface of the water. What she saw was the most amazing sight in the whole world. She was looking up at a huge waterfall. The view was breathtaking. It took everything in her to stay calm. She looked around. The landscape was amazingly rich with every color. Wherever she looked she saw all shades of green, yellow, orange, and red. It was wondrous. A pleasant breeze was caressing her. Her first thought was that she had reached heaven.

She looked at the sky and wondered, was it the same sky as in her waking life too. Suddenly a delight rushed in and overwhelmed her. It was explosive. After a while there was only stillness, pure stillness of being. She thought of her childhood when she had no fear, no desire, no ambition, yet she was happy all the time. It felt the same.

Then, she felt a presence as if someone was watching her, was aware that she was there. She looked around. There was no one. After a while, from the corner of the eye, she saw a movement behind a big tree on the right side of the hill. She saw a woman coming towards her. The woman's face caught her attention. It was the most beautiful face she had ever seen. Love and joy was radiating from her in all directions. Radha was so stunned by the woman's striking beauty that it took her a moment to realize she was staring.

"What does it mean to be successful in life?" the woman asked as if she had known Radha all her life and was continuing an old conversation. Her voice seemed familiar. "Does it not mean absence of failure?"

Radha said knowingly, speaking from her recent experience and consequent understanding, "If I am not a failure, then I can say I am successful. Success itself does not have any independent existence whatsoever."

"And you spend your life in pursuing something which does not exist independently and call yourself sane and, even, intellectual being," the woman said pleasantly.

"Then, I should not ask pleasant things in my life?" Radha asked mystified.

"You see, throughout your life you are in search of the pleasant, and you *do* get it; it is always followed by the unpleasant. Pursuit of happiness is the motivation in all of your—everyone's—actions. Your fault lies in avoiding the unpleasant. You have to understand that with pleasant you have to simultaneously accept pain, for both are different sides of the same coin. It is impossible to avoid sorrow if you wish to entertain joy."

"Something like, I have to accept thorns if I want to enjoy roses," Radha added sadly.

The woman said tenderly, "There is no other way. Good cannot exist without the bad. It needs the other to exist. Pain is a necessary condition to experience the joy of well-being. To enjoy food, it is not only important but necessary that you be hungry first. No matter how delicious the food is, you would not be able to really enjoy if you are not hungry. Any joy or sorrow comes with its opposite; otherwise, there is nothing called joy and nothing called sorrow. They complete each other like two wings of the same bird."

Radha looked around. In a flash, she saw that the landscape had magically transformed itself into the one covered with snow. Wherever she looked she saw snow, pure and eternal. There was a single red flower protruding out from behind a rock. The redness of the flower dominated the pureness of snow. Just a dot of red and what an astonishing effect it had! She became aware of the red as well as the white in a startling way.

The woman said softly, as if whispering a secret in her ears, "No pleasure in this world can satisfy you completely, because the pleasure, as normally understood, does not exist."

"What do you mean?"

"Pleasure is an effect produced by a cause. If the cause is real, then the effect would be real. You are pushed and pulled by the forces beyond your control. Hunger, thirst, cold, and heat have overwhelming effect on your physical existence. You have a deep longing for something permanent—that you look for in the relationships of parent, spouse, children, and friends; a need to be respected and well-placed in life. These physical, psychological, and social conditions deeply influence your so called joys and sorrows. On top of that, there is natural set up of things, like keeping the balance and harmony in nature. Any imbalance in nature is manifested as natural calamities. These things exert overwhelming pressure from all sides, and yielding to a pressure results in pleasure."

Radha remembered the times she felt powerless before such conditions. At one time, ages ago, she believed the world revolved around her. But there were times when she felt cold and ran to the warmth of heat; when she felt hunger and fled to the comfort of food; *and* when she looked for acknowledgement from peers. At such times she felt dwarfed by forces beyond her control. She could adjust the thermostat in her house, eat to satisfy hunger, take some action to win love and recognition from family and friends, but she could not conquer the conditions dominating her. She felt she was being mocked at by nature. Being aware and accepting the facts that there were things higher and beyond her control was the beginning of her quest, her need to reach to the end, or to the beginning.

"You remember the universe," the woman said, "only when there is some sort of natural calamity. You ignore what you don't understand and that's what you do in all aspects of your life. Yes, you have gone to the moon but still are not able to know why the heart in your body beats. Why the phenomenon of breath is working within. It is as it is, as it has always been. You have no control of something so close as your own heartbeat. You don't even want to know, because it reminds you of your own individual insignificance, of forces much bigger than you. You feel scared, so you close the eyes and pretend it does not affect you.

"You experience relief when you put down a heavy bag. You call this happiness." The woman continued without stopping, "If absence of weight is the cause of your happiness, then everyone should be happy because there is no weight on their backs. But no one is happy. That is the point."

Listening to the woman Radha felt she found a treasure. She wasn't looking for it, she wasn't even aware of its existence till just a moment ago.

"Don't you see the illusion? You have to put a pressure on yourself and then remove it. Immediately you will feel happy. It is not the absence of pressure but release from it that causes joy. A pressure is kept on your entire mind body complex by social, biological, and natural conditions. Whenever there is an urge, freedom from it brings satisfaction. When you are angry, Shouting brings some kind of release when you are angry; sight of food brings happiness when you are hungry."

"This is not freedom," Radha observed aloud. She felt good to have found a way to fit two pieces of the puzzle together. There still remained the rest of the puzzle to be solved.

"It shows you are utter slave to different urges that arise within you only," she said, never taking her eyes off Radha. "You succumb to them. Intense hunger, thirst, cold, and heat overwhelm you; like, dislike, love, and hatred stir your being, and you begin to react as opposed to thinking objectively. Reaction brings instant release."

"It is strange that slavishness gives me an impression of joy," Radha felt guilty.

"Strange indeed, it is an illusion. All experiences are relative. The pleasure or pain is only a sensation, a reaction of your sense organs to different objects, people, and situations in your life, which varies according to different moods of your mind."

"It is hard to digest, even though it makes sense intellectually." Radha pressed further, "Then, what is real?"

"Real should be universal. It should be valid at all times and circumstances, should not undergo any modification or be subject to contradiction; it should remain the same in the past, present, and future, as a wise person once said," the woman explained. There was tenderness in her voice as she continued further, "You don't know what is real, but you do know what is not real. Your joys are not real, your sorrows are not real, your triumphs are not real, and your defeats are not real."

"Then, I am not real, you are not real," Radha bursted out.

The woman didn't speak. She smiled, waiting.

"My joys and sorrows are real, at least to me," Radha added.

"You said it—at least to you. You cannot enjoy your favorite things if you are ill. If pleasant things are really pleasant, they should be pleasant at all times even when you are ill."

A deep sadness enveloped Radha, as she realized the truth in her words.

"Moreover, it should be equally pleasant to everyone. It is a known fact that everyone does not like the same thing. The things which gives you joy should give others also the same joy, and the things which threaten to consume you with sorrow should also give equal sorrow to others—that is, if your joys and sorrows are real."

Radha was so dazed she had to sit down.

"Every experience is relative, every sensation is changing. See through the illusion. The world is only a field where *you* experience *your* own reactions to *your* own choices and actions," the woman concluded.

Radha looked around but she couldn't see the woman anywhere. She had disappeared.

It had begun to snow and instead of feeling cold, Radha was feeling a strange sensation of lightness, accompanied by a kind of pleasure starting from the tip of her toes and slowly spreading upwards, like insects crawling on her body, except it didn't feel disturbing, but intoxicating. A veil fell off from her mind in an instant. She was left mesmerized at the truth which hid behind and, now, flashed forth as clear as the sun in clear sky. She realized with utmost clarity, not as an intellectual idea, that life comes in opposites. Up and down, good and bad, life and death. In her ceaseless endeavor to eliminate the negative she ignored to see that the positive is defined entirely in terms of the negative. Without darkness, she could not recognize light. One cannot exist without the other. Can a crest exist without the trough? Can love exist without hate or life without death? To destroy the negative is to destroy all possibility of the positive.

≈ **8** ≈

The Secret of Happiness

"The God separated a spirit from Himself and fashioned it into Beauty. He showered upon her all the blessings of gracefulness and kindness. He gave her the cup of happiness and said, "Drink not from this cup unless you forget the past and the future, for happiness is naught but the moment." —Khalil Gibran

Radha found herself walking on the snow. She was looking to find some familiar landmarks. Everything was covered with snow. There was not another soul in sight yet everything was more alive and throbbing than ever. Then, she saw the woman. She was looking at her intensely, waiting. Radha walked towards her with a pounding heart. She knew she was a step closer to unraveling the mystery of happiness. It gave her goose bumps.

"Then what is happiness? Why do I want nothing but personal gratification that comes from fulfilling my deep-seated desires and longings?" Radha asked, with confidence in the woman's knowledge.

"Do you ever wonder why you desire, why there are longings in the heart? Why anybody does any activity at all?"

"It feels good to be doing something, contributing to the growth of society," Radha answered.

"There is a bliss you seek in every endeavor of yours, whether it's ordinary things in life or bigger pursuits. Your life is a movement towards delight. But where is this bliss?"

Radha stood there, motionless. A slightest shift and everything would vanish.

"In objects of my desire," replied Radha.

"Are you sure?"

"I am not sure of anything now."

"Try."

"Well, if every effort is motivated by happiness, then happiness should be in the things desired and actions initiated for their fulfillment," she said, feeing like an intellect.

"You are conditioned to think that happiness is an achievement through effort in the direction of the things desired, just because you experience happiness upon possession of those things."

Radha felt the woman was speaking an alien language. The whole world knew happiness was attained by fulfilling desires. It is not something she heard from others but knows it from experience. Whenever she possessed a desired thing she felt happy, each and every time.

The woman looked at Radha and said, "Don't you find it strange that different people, in their urge towards happiness, have different objects of desire. A desire could be anything—a beloved, a child, wealth, fame, and so on. The principle of happiness seems to be present in every object since every object is the target of some subject or the other in this world. At the same time, this goodness feeling does not last forever. If a single thing cannot attract everyone's attention at the same time, it also cannot sustain one's attention forever. Desires change with changing circumstances. You cannot love or hate the same thing for eternity. If you have lived in a house for a long time, you desire to live in a different house—not because there is something wrong with the house, but because you long for something new."

They both stood there locked in a gaze too intimate to even describe. No one moved; everything stood still around them, outside as well as inside.

"But, money is a different story," Radha said.

"Why?"

"Everyone likes money. Who wouldn't enjoy having ten million dollars?" Radha asked innocently.

"The one who has 100 million dollars"

Radha was amazed at the wisdom that came out of her mouth. The woman simply was knowledge.

"I get it. Everything is relative."

"The entire life is a Phantasma; it is all a chimera," she said with unparallel authority. "There comes a time, maybe after a week or a year, when something happens and you are not going to feel so good. Maybe you have spent those 10 million dollars, or the accomplishment you felt at doing an action no longer entices you. A very interesting phenomenon takes place in this fulfillment of desires."

"There is more..."

"It further excites an additional desire and then another. This goes on endlessly till you are totally exhausted and defeated."

"Yes," Radha said deep in thought.

"If happiness comes from possessions of desirable things, then all wealthy people would be happy to the brim. Ask any one of the affluent and successful. All of them will tell you that they lead a comfortable life, but happy—that's a different story."

"I feel happy for some time. Then I'd begin to question it, for it did not bring such great pleasure as I had anticipated and, the joy would reduce with every moment. It has an end, just like it has a beginning." Radha added from experience.

"There is a story to demonstrate the point. Once, a wealthy man lived in this world. He wasn't always wealthy, but he worked hard and used his intelligence. Over the years, he became an outstandingly wealthy man. At first, he thought if only he could buy a house, he would be happy. He worked hard and, finally, was able to buy a house. Not just any house but the house of his dreams with everything in it. He was ecstatic. Then, once he moved in the house he realized the need to buy furniture and other things for the house. If only he could afford the furniture and latest electronics of his choice, he would be the happiest man on earth, he imagined. Again, he worked hard and bought whatever he wished for and much more. The house was filled with things."

"I can imagine his happiness. Not everyone is so lucky," Radha interrupted.

"He deserved it. He worked hard for it," the woman added.

"I have a feeling, it's not the end."

"He enjoyed the house for a while, and then began to think—if only I had the latest car to go with the house. He bought the latest car, then another; he finally ended up having a fleet of cars—Jaguar, Bentley, Rolls Royce and what not. Yet he was not satisfied. He would be happy but for some time, and then a new desire would arise. He wanted to own an aircraft to travel. Then a whole planet."

"You are making it up. No one owns a planet."

There was a serene expression on the woman's face as she said, "You are missing the point. Desire is a bottomless bucket. You keep on filling it, still it remains empty. Today you want this, tomorrow you want that, and it goes on forever. True happiness cannot be found in the objects of desire. That's the point. You are looking at all the wrong places. It is a big illusion. You need to stop for a moment and make an attempt to understand the structure of things. No matter what you desire or how hard you work to make it happen, you always feel there is something more. It is not as great as you had imagined. But, you also know from experience that no amount of possessions can satisfy this insatiable hunger for more and more."

"Then where is it?—if not in the objects of the world. May be in my mind? It is said happiness is a state of mind," Radha was becoming restless.

"If happiness is a state of mind, then there is no point in you moving towards the things of the world for joy. The fact that you are unsatisfied and feel an obligation to move towards the world shows that something is lacking in the mind itself. A void is always felt. Your heart speaks a language you cannot explain. There is a flaw in thinking that happiness is a state of mind."

"But it must be somewhere." Radha felt she was on a treasure-hunt.

"This is the greatest secret. The entire world of perception is the alliance of the subject and objects. You cannot find happiness in the mind (subject) or in the things of world (objects)." There was a mischievous look in her eyes.

"Where is it?" Radha was too excited to contain herself.

"It is right in front of you if you can only stop making stories filled with concepts and ideas; actually within you. You are standing on the treasure of joy and looking for it everywhere," she said solving the riddle.

The time froze for Radha.

"I need more elaboration. My small mind with its limited understanding cannot comprehend," Radha implored.

"First, the gratification that you feel by possessing your desired things is not real, because possession itself is not real. It is a big deception."

Radha felt she was going to explode.

"You need to shift your way of looking slightly to see that things cannot be really possessed by anyone since everything is arranged in the world at separate and distinct points in space and time as external objects. The idea of possession is such a strange idea. It is only a social arrangement of values—material or psychological—agreed by people, as an accepted state of affairs. It is valid as long as all agree about it. It is a big facade."

"That's right. My values rearrange according to my circumstances as a community. Values have changed with changing times. Different parts of the world have different views of themselves. In some place, just surviving is considered luxurious whereas in another place, even living a luxurious life is not satisfactory. What was unthinkable yesterday is totally acceptable today, and perhaps tomorrow it may again change." Radha was surprised at her own spontaneous answer.

"When you pour water from two different glasses into one bigger glass, they merge with each other," the woman explained. "When two colors are mixed, they merge together to form a different color. That's what possession should mean in real terms—getting united with the desired thing, truly and totally. You cannot merge with the desired things no matter how dear they are to the heart. Your house, your property, your spouse, your friends, your children; everyone is outside you. You can own a house, you can live in it, but you cannot merge with it. Hence, nothing in the world can be permanently possessed."

It had again begun to snow lightly, the silence pregnant with all that would or could happen. Nothing moved, not Radha, not the woman, not a leaf, nothing except snow falling down in its softness. For a moment, there was only the stillness of silence which captured the beauty of the mountains, of Radha, of the woman; ultimately of the existence, not as it can be captured but in an unfathomable way captured in time, frozen with infinite potentiality.

"That is why the wealthy man was so restless because of his inability to merge with his house, cars, and planet." Radha was scintillating with insight.

The woman spoke, "Happiness is an existence; it is everywhere—unconditional and unrelated. It has nothing to do with the possession of things. You may possess or you may not possess. Even millions and millions of finite things put together remain finite in the end."

Radha felt the magnitude of the woman's words. She was unable to grasp her mind's inability to see through the thick veil of stories, "If all this is a phantom of mind, why does it stir my being with such an overwhelming intensity? Something imaginary cannot beckon me with such power that I become its slave."

Her face was glowing more and more with every passing moment.

"Things appear desirable because you feel there is something in them capable of giving you happiness."

"But you just explained that happiness is not dependent on possessions of things. Now I am confused."

The woman's eyes shone with mischief. "This happiness is artificially brought about by an apparent union between the subject and the object. It is neither real nor permanent."

Radha thought of countless times in her life when she desired one thing or another. As a child she had desired new toys on the market. As a teenager she had desired attention from her peers. As a grownup she had desired so many different things at different times, it was difficult to even remember. Every time she felt happy whenever she got the things she desired. At the same time she wondered how come at different times, different things gave her happiness. It was not possession of things but her desires which gave the things the power to make her happy. By themselves, things were neutral.

"Have you ever wondered—what is the mind which desires, feels that something is lacking." She paused momentarily before continued further. "It is an intensely focused form of consciousness. Any particular arrangement of consciousness in space and time can be said to be a mind, human or otherwise."

"Hold on. Any particular arrangement of consciousness in space and time can be said to be a mind, human or otherwise!" Radha repeated, trying to comprehend.

"When water is poured in a vessel, it takes the shape of the vessel. If the glass is tall, water looks tall. If the glass is wide, water looks wide. Though the water is same, it looks like and gets restricted to the shape of the glass. In the same way, when consciousness takes the shape of a mind, it feels and, therefore, gets limited to the boundaries created by that mind—due to it being focused. Consciousness is indivisible and whole, but, somehow, it alienates itself in the form of a particular mind, one that believes itself to be in possession of certain characteristics and not others."

"Explain more please."

"When you say there is a thing called 'green,' it automatically means there are other things which are not 'green'. 'Green' has alienated from other colors. When white light is focused through a glass, it becomes separated into different colors. Imagine if one color becomes self-aware and thinks that it is only that color and nothing else, that it is distinct from all other colors in the spectrum, while it is part of white light— and all other colors are part of white light too. Together they are the white light. You can say that this particular color is an intensely focused form of white light. When Consciousness is similarly focused, it becomes aware of other minds which appear to be distinct from each other, and a boundary is created by it only, the boundary of 'I' and the rest of the world. If there is 'this mind', there are simultaneous possibilities—infinite in number—of 'other minds' which are not 'this mind'. The phenomenon due to which Consciousness gets focused is called self-affirmative tendency or, in simple terms, Ego. It is individual consciousness as opposed to universal consciousness, focused consciousness as opposed to consciousness. We will talk about it later in detail. For now it means: if there exists Radha, there are also others who are not Radha."

Radha became more alive than ever. She felt glorious with the knowledge pouring on her.

"Any form of particularization is finite and this is the source of restlessness. You imagine that a certain object, a certain person, or a certain event has characteristics which complement your particularization, and you try to possess them. When it is possessed, a sensation of completeness is experienced."

"Just like when I solve a puzzle. I try to fit two shapes together. When I find the perfect fit, I feel happy," Radha added.

"But as soon as you match a pair, you become aware that there are other parts too which needs to be matched to complete the puzzle. The world is made in such a way that there are infinite varieties of finiteness; everything is related to everything else. In the cosmic setup, puzzle pieces are never exhausted. You feel happy for some time only, because soon you recognize a new limitation in relation to the existing possession. Every experience of happiness in the world is therefore fleeting."

A strange exquisite bird with blue feathers flew by, catching Radha's attention. It flew over and circled the woman and Radha before flying away. A magnificent rainbow had formed throwing brilliant colors in the sky. Radha's heart skipped a beat. She gasped at its dazzling perfection, looked at it in open wonder that such a thing could be. Movement was life, stillness was divine.

"Like the wealthy man who couldn't stop desires from piling up in the living room of his mind. First, the house, then furniture, then cars and spacecraft, and finally a whole planet," Radha couldn't help but see the image of a distraught man sitting on a remote planet with a restless face. She found his story poignant and couldn't shake him off.

The woman spoke further, "You are so absorbed in completing the puzzle that you don't see you are not the puzzle pieces, but the stuff the puzzle is made of! In this cosmic play, you have divided yourself into different pieces. You are not just a particular color but the stuff color is made of.

"The mysterious phenomenon behind the world, which suggests the attainability of happiness, is a profound subject that has intrigued ages and ages of generations ranging from: ordinary people to philosophers, intellectuals, psychologists, and great minds in the field of purely objective science, alike. Every soul yearns for happiness; every mind wants to know the source of it. It is the same subject discussed in ancient scriptures where our ancestors pondered upon the mystery of

Existence. When religion talks about God, it is talking about the same mysterious Presence hidden in the things of the world as well as the world itself. When enlightened masters talk, they are talking about the same Presence which is divinely present everywhere—due to which one can have a glimpse of happiness. This Presence has made sane people go completely insane in mad ecstasy over the mystical union of the subject and object. It is the same divine Principle which is present behind your existence, my existence."

Radha was feeling intoxicated without any alcohol. Her heart was throbbing with new energy.

"You want to know the source of happiness—then look within. You will find it in the deepest chamber of your heart. Hear it in the delight of a bird, feel it in the flight of a kite, and touch it in the blooming of a flower. See it in the beauty of the butterfly, taste it in the sweetness of honey, and live it in your own breath. It is the foundation of your being. You are filled to the brim with joy.

"Just like you get ice cubes by freezing water; you can put water in trays of different shape and sizes. You can have infinite number of ice cubes. But they are basically water, simple and pure. No matter how much you feel you are finite and separate from the rest, it does not change the reality that you are like water, one and the same, full of joy, dividing yourself into the subject and object for the sake of experience—so that the universal becomes infinite particulars and play the game of life."

An unending joy was radiating from the woman, carrying Radha in its sweet warmth. She became aware of herself being cuddled by the entire existence. Radha was beginning to dance, slow rhythmic movements over which she had no control. She was bursting with a delight—a completeness she never thought was possible. After a moment of silence, in which Radha experienced a flash which threatened to smash her mind like an earthquake, the woman spoke again.

"Your love for things is, in truth, your love towards perfection and completeness. You love completeness of being, imagined to be present in the possession of things. You have misunderstood the whole point— even when you are clinging to your material possessions."

"Yes, yes!" Radha said, tears of joy rolling down her eyes.

"Your ceaseless movement towards happiness is self revealing by demonstrating that you are not satisfied with any amount of happiness which is finite by nature. The source of happiness is not in the things desired but hides in your own depths. It is all light and perfection."

"Yes!" Radha felt in a moment she would explode, and her body be thrown into pieces.

There was reverence in the woman's voice. "This bliss is near to you, nearer than your own mind and breath. It already exists within the sacred spaces of your being! All the wealth of this world—and of seven worlds—is not going to give you something which you already have: fulfillment. You are always full and complete, everywhere, at all times. What pulls you in the direction of an object is not the object but the universal hidden inside—for the object is a subject in its own status, and its essence is as much a center of consciousness as your own subjectivity. A reflection cannot satisfy you, only the real thing can. And you are the real thing. When you start looking inside instead of projecting yourself outside as desires, then you will know what you are: a wholeness"

The woman began dancing, and her face became more and more radiant till Radha could not see her but only a dazzling light resonating with love and joy which, before she could think, entered her.

"At the peak of an experience, you cease to exist and experience something beyond any words." She reappeared and continued speaking. "When you are captured by natural beauty, when you touch the heights of success, when you are in a beloved's embrace—you forget yourself. It is simply merging in joy. You become joy. There is no I, no you, no object—nothing. It is just bliss bursting forth. The bliss felt then already exist within you. It is revealed when individualities are thrown in oblivion and wholesome togetherness is embraced. The boundaries of separate entities melt, even if for a moment. It is a profound moment where time stands still, and you remain totally absorbed in the territory of here and now.

"Are these moments the gateway to reality?"

"What is experienced in this holy moment is not even the tip of an iceberg. It is only a faint recognition of something beyond the known. It is a glimpse, not the whole thing."

"Not even the tip of an iceberg."

Radha started dancing again. The woman was disappearing as Radha was expanding. She felt an explosion and found herself full of bliss. She wondered how such a thing could be. It was not an orgasm as is normally understood, but so much more than that. Her whole being was dancing in orgasmic bliss; there was a simultaneous thrill throughout. It didn't originate from any point—there was no epicenter—but came from the unknown unfathomable depths within. From the tip of her toes to the top of her head, pleasure was everywhere. No word could capture it. It wasn't just her; she felt that each and every particle of the cosmos was dancing in orgasmic bliss at all times. She just became aware of it and it took her in its embrace throwing her into infinite ecstasy. The woman was right. It was not even the tip of an iceberg.

≈ **9** ≈

Manifesting desires

"Child, I have forgotten the art of being absorbed in sticks and mud-pies. I seek out costly playthings, and gather lumps of gold and silver. With whatever you find you create your glad games, I spend both my time and my strength over things I never can obtain. In my frail canoe I struggle to cross the sea of desire, and forget that I too am playing a game" —Rabindranath Tagore

After a moment or an eternity—she lost track of time—Radha became aware of herself again. She could hear the tick tocks of the clock on the right wall, and she could hear the stillness of the night, breathing. The woman was still there looking compassionately at her, also with reverence—the state Radha had just experienced was extraordinary and glorious.

"What is the meaning of life then? It is not possible—not to desire and wish. That would be repressing," Radha asked like a child, who was learning letters and numbers.

The woman looked relaxed than ever, with peace descending on everything around her.

"Do not repress anything, my friend, but desire fully and consciously; desire with all your heart and soul. Worship your desires, for they are the gifts from the divine. Embrace them, for they are a touch from your beloved. Adore them, for they are the innocence of a child, and surrender to them, for in them is hidden the answer to your prayers. Universe delights to give you what you wish for. What's the fun in living if there were no longings in the heart. There is no meaning in life if you don't *create* it. It is a painting that you paint, a song that you sing, a story that you write. It is an understanding that you bring through your consciousness. So, create a life of joy and abundance."

"Creation is the purpose. This is huge."

"But make desires your friends, not enemies," she continued, "treat them as playmates. Be their masters, not slaves. Fill the heart with gratitude, instead of complains. Be happy that you have so many toys to play with. You are the player. New desires mean new toys in the market. Do not become the toys. See through the illusion. Think of it like this: when a mirage is seen you think that the water is near, and that it will quench your thirst. Once you know it is an optical illusion, you will still see the mirage but see it as mirage not water. Nothing in the world has the capacity to quench your thirst except you, simply because you are the water. See the beauty of life and the fun of living when you begin to create for the simple pleasure of experience and the pure joy of expression; when you treat desires as friendly playthings, not monsters that wreck havoc on your heart and mind."

"How"

"Be always aware of the process going on. Understand the dynamics of desire and action. Be aware that you desire this, and when you work towards its fulfillment—be aware that you are moving towards its fulfillment. Always see them as passing clouds. Now this desire is coming, let it come. Watch it like a movie. Do not react by attaching any value to it. In a movie, you do not crave for things to happen your way and if it doesn't happen, you do not become averse to it. You just watch."

"What process? I need more explanation," Radha said.

"Every urge, every desire manifests into action. There is no other way to live but through performance of action. Something needs to be done, something needs to be desired. How often do you not do anything and feel satisfied? You are not satisfied with simply existing. You want to change, to become. Your whole life is an action to achieve an end. These are the creative tools you have at your disposal at all times. If a painter chooses to paint, then imagine the strokes of the brush to be the actions performed. Working behind the action of the painter is the imagination and the desire to paint—painter's thoughts, beliefs, and choices. A desire always comes first, followed by corresponding action.

"Yes,—action is the expression of desire."

"Listen to this phenomenal truth. Know it in your heart. Fulfillment is the natural course taken by a desire. There is nothing more you can do. For example, a desire arises in your mind to drink hot water. You can do as much as putting the water in pot, pot on stove, and fire underneath the stove. Doing all this is the action you perform. Beyond that, water will boil itself in few minutes. There is a natural process working in the background—of fire. Heat is inherent in fire. You do not question the ability of the fire to heat the water. Similarly, there is a process working in the background, though invisible to you, but there, making your desires move towards their fulfillment. It is effortless beyond this point."

"Effortless. I am hearing this lot."

"Deeper truths of the cosmos can be grasped through metaphors and stories; they help to put a point across which is otherwise impossible to understand. Suppose you start wondering why it is taking so long for water to boil; unnecessary you worry. The only thing required is waiting and watching—if you get distracted then it is possible that all water may evaporate, or you may spill it and burn your hand. Attention is very important. You cannot blame fire for burning you. The fire that cooks food is the same fire that burns a house. A force is a force. It can build, or it can destroy. How you use it is entirely up to you. It is not fire's fault that you were not attentive and burned your house cooking."

"Incredible."

"Let's look at it to understand the dynamics of desire and action. You would not have performed the action of heating the water if the desire to drink hot water was not there. So, it all begins with a desire— a desire to drink water or a desire to bring a change to the world. And then action is the most natural thing to do. You don't wait for some magical power to come and give you hot water while you do nothing, only wishing and expecting—and then complain that you are a victim; life is not fair to you. Do you see how ridiculous it is?"

"It's not going to work." Radha smiled.

"You just have to do appropriate actions and leave the rest to the process. Do not create unnecessary drama by worrying. Have patience, give some time for the process to do the work, but remain alert and observe in a playful manner. You just keep an eye on them now and then.

"One important thing to remember is that the fire did the job, though the action of putting the water on the stove was initiated by you. Do not think that the water boiled because of your efforts. Desires do not get fulfilled just because you made an effort. Those are necessary actions, but they do not completely do the job. The process behind it is absolutely necessary. Do not puff your ego by thinking—'I am doing this, I did that.' You planted a seed, now nature will do the rest. Though planting a seed is absolutely necessary, it must be in fertile soil. Respect the process," she said watching Radha with an odd expression of a teacher teaching a new concept, who expected a lot of skepticism.

"This is difficult," Radha said. "First you said your choices define your actions and are responsible for the kind of life you live. And now you are saying that your actions are not important. This is disempowering. This means I have no free will." Radha was surprised that she didn't feel disempowered at all.

"This is a good sign. It means you are paying attention. Questions are absolutely necessary to grasp an idea before you can finally accept. Again, I ask you not to fall into the trap of words. Do you think that a child is disempowered if he (she) surrenders himself to his mother (or father)? Mother knows how to take care of her child. The child wants to jump from the top of a building, just because it seems exciting and adventurous. Do you think, stopping him means disempowering him. His act of standing on the edge of the window with an intention to jump is his action propelled by his desire to jump. Before he could jump, the mother comes and pulls him in. The child cries because his desire remains unfulfilled. The mother tries to make him understand that he would have got hurt badly or even die if he jumped. The child doesn't understand because he is a child. His understanding is not so developed. He becomes sad and miserable."

Radha was speechless, her eyes filled with inexplicable wonder.

"Do you think that the child is nothing to the mother?" she asked Radha.

"No." Radha smiled as she thought of Abhi and Anya and the tremendous power they had on her and Suraj. Everything ceased to exist in front of them; only they remain, and love.

"He is everything to the mother. She loves him with all her heart and soul. In fact, children have more control over their parents, and they manipulate them because of this weakness of love."

"Till the time his intelligence is developed enough, she does the best she can to make him comfortable and loved. She tries to fulfill every wish he has, even the unreasonable and whimsical ones, out of love. If the child cries every time the mother washes his face, she is not disempowering him. She is practicing hygiene. She reasons with him, setting the limits so that he does not become a totally irresponsible person. If the situation demands it, time out is given. No one likes time out, but it is a necessary and useful tool."

Radha felt like a child looked after by a loving mother called life. She felt embraced and loved by the whole cosmos.

"All sad times in life—my tragedies and failures—are basically life washing my face or giving me time out for my own good," she said.

"Within the safe limits, the child has the freedom to do whatever he wants," the woman replied. "He can run in the yard, play games. He then starts playing something else, whatever catches his whim and fancy. The possibilities are endless. The mother keeps an eye on him even when he thinks she is not watching. But the mother knows everything and doesn't rebuke him or his silly games because she knows it is only a game he is playing. At the end of the day, he will come back to her."

"Are you saying that my actions are but playing games as a child does in the backyard?" Radha asked incredulously.

"Sometimes you cry, sometimes you laugh, sometimes you create, sometimes you destroy; all the time thinking you are doing something. Sure, you are doing something very worthwhile. You are creating, expressing, and experiencing. This is the purpose of creation. But see through the maze of desiring and fulfilling them. They are the games you play to keep yourself busy. In the beginning you know it is a game. But somewhere after that, you begin to experience joy or sorrow attached to the wrong identification with the game. You forget about your life, house, mother, father, everything—and the game becomes your reality. Then all misery follows. Play, but play for the joy of playing, for the love of creation. Do not read meaning into it."

"Why doesn't the mother make me remember?" Radha felt like a research student.

"The mother has lot of chores to do around the house. She would come and let you know the game is over when her chores are done, or when it is time to wrap up the games. As it is, you are so wrapped up in your games you are not missing her."

"Does the mother not mind?"

"Do you mind when your kids play?"

"No, Stimulation and interaction—games—are absolutely necessary for children to grow and evolve. They are part of the education." Understanding hit her as she answered her own question. "But there has to be a way out of this circle of playing and forgetting?"

"When suddenly a sweet remembrance flashes in your mind about your mother's presence, you become aware of your true identity. The mother leaves everything and comes to you. All you have to do is remember her, cry out her name."

"Who is the mother?" Radha could not keep her curiosity quiet.

"Who do you think?"

"I don't know?"

"The mother is not different from you. You are included in her. Since your understanding is not so developed, I have taken the analogy of the mother and child. She is your own higher self. She is the divine principle, the mysterious presence behind each and everything, the core of your being. Call it God, Spirit, Witness, Pure Subjectivity."

Suddenly Radha felt herself falling deeper into some depths. The depths kept on throwing her into the heights, filling her with fear and excitement—both rolled into one. Then deep sleep came over her.

Radha woke up in the middle of the night. Everything was quite and still. The woman's words ringing in her ears. *Just watch your desires, do not identify with them, the effortless process in the background, the mother looking after her child.* She was feeling sleepy. She would think about it in the morning. Before a moment passed she fell asleep again and found herself inside the hollow space of the sacred tree. The monk was watching over her, smiling.

"I don't understand. If I am not attached to my desires, how can I begin to work towards their fulfillment? Where is the motivation or the fun?" Radha continued the conversation she was having with the woman as if he was also present earlier.

He looked at her in a way which reminded her of her own Guruji in the Ashram, compassionate and kind. "Desires are there because you don't understand your relationship with the objects of desire. When you become a witness and watch your desires like a play, they will begin to unravel themselves and reveal their true identity, and also your identity. Desires are intelligent and know how to fulfill themselves. In the meantime, all you have to do is enjoy and allow the process to take its own course."

"I know the process," Radha said.

"It takes a while for this kind of knowledge to mature. First, you hear about it. Then, you reflect on it. Do not accept it just because someone said so. Experience it within yourself as reality. Know it for sure. The only way to experience it is by remaining totally objective. Watch your next desire as you watch a car on the road. Observe like a doctor observes a patient, always retaining his knowledge and identity as a doctor. A doctor does not identify with the patient. If he does, it becomes impossible for him to give an effective cure."

Radha was so enthralled, she wanted him to go on and not stop speaking. Wisdom was coming out of his mouth, and she felt carried away in its embrace.

"Everything is put there as a stage for you to enact different parts. If the actor becomes attached to his role and begins reacting to situations, he, then, experiences various emotions attached to it. You would call him mad because he is reacting to things which are made up. But you do the same thing every moment of your life. You read meanings into things which are made up only. Imagine yourself to be an actor in a play, enjoy your part fully, conscious of your reality at all times but convincing enough, true to your part. Then see the joy of living. Life becomes an instrument of creation, of experience, and of love, compassion, and joy," he said with the utmost calm expression.

"Why is it important to understand all this? I have more pressing and real physical, social, and political needs. They exert overwhelming pressure on me," she asked.

"All these needs begin from and end at understanding life and how it works, if you look at it in right light," he began to explain. "Philosophical and spiritual quest is also about understanding life. If you like cakes, imagine them to be various needs in your system. Your actions are motivated by them, and you are always working to fulfill them. Your spiritual need is learning that all these different cakes are made of flour and a few other ingredients. By knowing the process of mixing and cooking you can not only make cakes, but also many other things which you didn't even know existed before; infinite possibilities for infinite life. By understanding you can use few ingredients in different ways and live a more fulfilled life than you can ever imagine. To say that you only like cake and don't care about other things, you are depriving yourself of an enriching life. For what is cake without sugar, and what is life without awareness."

His words made her think profoundly. She was feeling an expansion within and felt that she would be able to jump out of her body if she tried. She could jump from the top of the mountain and not get hurt if she tried, but she didn't dare try.

By the time she woke up next, it was early morning. She began to write. The conversation with the woman and monk was still fresh in her mind. She didn't want to lose the knowledge in the scattered activity of her mind. Words were bubbling inside her. A wide smile remained on her face the whole time she was writing:

Desire could be anything—a soul mate, a career, family, wealth, any or all of these. Within the structure of desire I can desire anything and everything. But why there are desires in my heart is a profound question. Understanding the answer to this question is important. I have longings for things which I have lost due to forgetfulness, but they are within only. Just like when I am wearing a watch on the wrist. I search for it everywhere, except where it really is—on my wrist. I am reflecting and projecting myself as desires. That is why when I fulfill them, any number of them, I do not get real fulfillment. I give external situations and events power over me. Due to some mysterious inexplicable power of projection and veiling prevalent in the universe uniformly, I don't see the whole picture. I get caught in my own net and feel victimized by circumstances. It is not possible to get infinite satisfaction from finite things. I want freedom from hunger, from thirst, from heat, from cold, and from longing itself. I wish to rise above the bondages felt within me. I am in pursuit of endless perfection. At the end of my mind there is a vague perception of something above and beyond me, transcending my present personality, and at the same time belonging to me.

As she finished writing, the meaning sunk more and more in the depth of her mind, and she experienced astonishing heights within.

PART TWO

Where the mind is without fear and

the head is held high.

Where knowledge is free

Where the world has not been broken up into

fragments by narrow domestic walls.

Where words come out from the depth of truth.

Where tireless striving stretches its arms towards

perfection.

Where the clear stream of reason has not lost its way

Into the dreary desert sand of dead habit.

Where the mind is led forward by thee

Into ever widening thought and action.

Into that heaven of freedom, my Father, let my country
awake.

-Rabindranath Tagore

≈ 10 ≈

The Story of 'I'

"Humans are divided into different clans and tribes, and belong to countries and towns. But I find myself a stranger to all communities and belong to no settlement. The Universe is my country and the human family is my tribe." — Khalil Gibran

Radha was immersed deep in thought and then she saw it. She stopped in her tracks. A full moon adorned the sky. She never saw the beauty before, though she had seen the moon a thousand times. She was left without a thought, and everything became new and brilliant: the moon, the night with innumerable stars, houses on the road — space caressing everything. As she stood mesmerized looking at the dazzling beauty of the moon, she became aware of an unfathomable depth into her being; a depth which was not part of her physical frame — like her height or width — but this depth of hers, she realized, was part of something vast and immeasurable, something which was ultimately incomprehensible to her mind. It belonged to another dimension her thoughts could not reach, neither could her intellect understand. Every part of her had become intensely still. Then the depth began expanding and exploding, coming in waves and throwing her beyond time and space, filling her with delight. She had become joy!

Later, she was relieved to find Suraj still sleeping besides her. He hadn't vanished as she had feared. She looked around. Everything was as it was yet everything had changed. She was surrounded with magnificence. She felt a surge of love rush in and wanted to hug the whole world. It couldn't be imaginary. How could she imagine what she had never felt before. It was beyond any emotion; all emotions were contained in it. It was a force. She felt touched by the divine. She realized there were realms of existence she knew nothing about, and now she knew that she didn't know.

As she closed her eyes, forms began to take shape in the space of her mind. Empty space of her mind became a canvas and on it came the snow-clad mountains, with the speed of a thought. Radha found herself facing the angelic woman with a tenderness she had not known.

"I have been waiting for you," she said.

"Who are you, and where am I?"

"It does not matter. Ask what you have to ask."

Radha was waiting with her questions. "Why do I give meaning to situations and people in my life? Why does it seem impossible not to react to perceptions?"

"You have asked a complicated yet the simplest of questions," the woman said. "It reveals a chain of questions. The answer to this becomes the next question, and all needs to be grasped upon before you can fully comprehend all the answers." She took a deep breath and continued, "There is an inscrutable phenomenon working in the cosmos uniformly. It is called *ego* or, in other words, 'I'. It is because of *it* that you have perception of anything at all. It is the beginning. If you didn't have ego, you wouldn't perceive anything. If you don't perceive anything, you won't read meanings into it."

"I..."

"Yes, it all begins with the birth of 'I', and everything about life is nothing but the story of 'I'. It is the ultimate deception—*ego* doesn't even exist. It just seems to exist because we believe it exists."

"My individuality is behind my blocked understanding...but there should be a way to see through it," Radha said.

"It is the most perplexing principle ever encountered. It is the self-alienating faculty in all of us and compels one to affirm that 'I am this or that' and 'this is what I want'. Consider again the case of colors in white light and how a phenomenon is working to isolate white into different colors. Ego is the same phenomenon forcing *consciousness* to become focused. What it is, how it is created—nobody knows. *And* it forces everyone to act in a particular way."

"...in self-interest."

"Yes. The fact that you are distinct from others, your confidence—a sense of your individual being—that you exist independent of others is the work of *ego*."

"My pride," Radha commented.

The woman voice was deep as she whispered the sublime secret, "Its essence is far more subtle than your 'pride'. It is a profound and complex subject. Ego has many layers going deeper and deeper into the mind, and its structure is not easy to understand. Its fundamental function is creating the boundary between 'I' and 'the rest of the world.' It is the first boundary created. Though it is imaginary, nothing can be more powerful. You have to apply your mind carefully or the meaning will be lost on you."

Radha was intrigued. She was totally absorbed in what the woman said.

"Whenever a boundary is created, there arise two opposites. When you draw a line on a blank page, it instantly divides the page into two distinct and opposite parts. Though the division is only by a line, its effect is overwhelming. Whoever looks at the paper would instantly become aware of the inevitable consequence of the paper being divided into two separate parts notwithstanding it is one whole paper."

"Yes. The brilliance of light can only be accentuated in darkness, as someone has said," Radha said with intellectual anticipation.

"When you become aware of your existence, simultaneously, you become aware of others existence who are not you. A boundary is being created instantly with far reaching effects. Every boundary line is a battle line since it is charged with a deep compulsion towards its survival at the cost of anything whatsoever in the world. It is the beginning of your conflict because alienation and fragmentation begins from here. Each *ego* feels itself to be separate from others and needs to protect itself from them. It is the most potent and cherished boundary since it is the first. Everything else stems from it only. Seeing, hearing, understanding, feeling, and all other psychological functions are various manifestations of a single impulse from inside to affirm oneself as distinct from others and, therefore, dominate over others. It is the split between you and the rest of the world, between the subject and the object."

She was looking at Radha with a gentle expression of wisdom, also reassuring in its own way.

Radha gaped at the woman—she who had come out of nowhere to dispel the darkness clouding her mind.

The woman continued in a patient and loving voice, "Countless other boundaries are created on the foundation of this one. The circle of 'I' gets wider and wider: myself, my children, my family, my community, my religion, my country, my planet. There is the social ego where one belongs to a certain status. There is the professional ego where one belongs to a particular skill like lawyer, doctor, and so on. There is cultural ego, political ego—there are countless distinctions extending to endless details. We fight as individuals; we fight as countries; we fight as religious communities. These wars are nothing but conflicts of egos; each ego wishing to assert itself as the fittest whether it is individual ego or group of egos."

"An illusion can be so strong!"

"Originally it exists as the principle of awareness, a simple consciousness that one *is*. But since it is necessary to experience the world from a point of view, as an inevitable consequence, *It* becomes aware of others as *'you,' 'him,' 'her,' 'this,' and 'that'*. Consciousness gets twisted. To make an analogy: one looks at a painting from a particular angle and another from another angle. Many people are looking at the same painting but have different views. They never feel it is the same painting, so intensely confident they are about their opinions. To take it further, they are not different people but different parts of the same painting which have, somehow, become self-aware and begin to identify with the parts and see themselves as distinct from others. They are not even aware that they are part of a bigger picture, so powerful is the effect of their ego. It is an addiction— me, mine, and I. This addiction is stronger than alcohol or any other substance. It becomes grosser and grosser till it reaches the most concrete of its expressions."

Radha looked at the woman and then she looked around. Wherever she looked she saw snow, infinite and eternal. There was not a footprint, not a single mark in the entire landscape, only the pureness and perfection of snow.

"Why and how I have come to affirm myself as such?" She asked.

"It is not possible to apprehend completely the process by which we have come to affirm ourselves as such. But it is the most necessary thing in creation. Without it, no creation can take place. We are always a person first, something else later. We have infinite possibilities, but we will always be a person first. Why we feel that we are individuals cannot be understood by us because our intellect is also a function of our individuality. We cannot know anything objectively if we are already a part of it. This is the whole problem," she said peacefully.

Radha stood still, her hands to her sides and looked into the woman's deep brown eyes, "—part of it?"

"To have complete understanding of a thing, we have to stand apart from it as an outsider and then look at it without prejudice. If a particular color has to have complete knowledge of the color white, it has to stand apart from the whole spectrum of light and then observe it objectively."

"It is not possible. When—if it is even possible—a particular color does observe the white light then the light changes due to the very absence of that particular color. Is it possible for the light to see itself completely?" Radha wondered aloud.

"How did you learn about the anatomy of frogs in high school?"

"Well, I dissected them, observed every part of their bodies before making any conclusions," she said carrying an intellectual air.

"If you were a part of that frog, would you have understood about it the way you understand now, as standing separate and looking at it as an object?"

"No."

"In the same way, it is not possible to understand *ego* because we exist in the present state through it. How can a cell in a body have correct understanding of the whole body? We are wearing the glasses of our individualities. To know *ego*, we have to transcend it. The mind that thinks, the intellect that grasps, or the reason that argues, are not sufficient. What can they think, understand, or argue but that which is within the boundary of intellect, not beyond."

"I need more explanation. My mind with its limited understanding fails to grasp the deeper meaning," Radha implored, mystified.

"Well, you agree that the mind precedes everything," the woman started again.

"Yes."

"It has few aspects. First is the thinking faculty. That part of the mind which has the capacity to understand is called intellect and is considered above and superior to the ordinary mind. When we become aware of the things around us as specifics, like a tree, a chair, or a person, it is called perception. When we grasp a particular situation, it's called understanding."

Radha had become absolutely still and quite. In that stillness of the mind, she became aware of a flash originating at a point within her. It left her startled.

"Then, something more significant happens. We choose to act upon our perception. Our whole being wells up based on our understanding to the existent situation, and we begin to feel, not merely perceive. This reaction is called emotion." The woman paused allowing enough time for Radha to follow. "Every perception is followed by a reaction. Whether it is a tree or a person, we have to pass an opinion on it— desirable or not. It is called reading meaning into a situation."

"Mind, intellect and ego; it cognizes, perceives, and reacts," Radha repeated to herself. She had started to take notes in her mind and was beginning to see through the trick of her mind. She regretted she hadn't brought a notebook.

"Again these are words only, to explain and understand. You have to be careful and not fall in their trap. These are various functions a mind performs. We have to understand that cognition, perception, reaction all are all rooted in the ego principle. It is the only level in any perception. The rest are details. Before I can understand and then react, I have to be sure that I exist. If I am not aware of myself as distinct from others, then there is no need to understand anything at all, simply because the other does not exist. There is nothing to perceive and react to," she spoke with amazing authority.

Radha stood there scared to move. She feared if she shifted even an inch, the knowledge pouring on her would vanish.

"Every time we try to comprehend the play of ego, mind, and intellect, we get entangled by the mind itself. Don't you see the dynamics of reaction and judgment?"

"It never crossed my mind."

"The final one is *the seat of consciousness*. It is the substance through which all faculties of the mind act, like the sea in which various faculties are waves. It is difficult to grasp this before we understand the first three: mind, intellect, and ego. We will come upon this later."

"Like awareness of my own presence."

"Let's take baby steps," the woman smiled.

"Then, why do I get torn apart from conflicting emotions? Why do I live my life searching for meanings in relationships, things, and situations?" Radha was frustrated at her inability to grasp fully.

"Questions may be many, but the answer is only one—because we react, because we judge. The seat of consciousness gets blurred by mental waves as we perceive or think anything. It, then, takes the shape of our thought, and we fall in the web of reactions and judgments. Why our consciousness takes the shape of our thought is also because of the individuality principle present within. No matter what route we take, we always come back to the ego because it is the beginning.

"Of what"

"Of the world, of Creation," the woman answered.

Radha knew she was a step closer in unraveling the mystery of life. She felt beyond gratitude, beyond any understanding of it. Lost in the bliss no drug can produce, Radha found herself looking into the woman's deep eyes, dazed by the effect she was having on her.

"We don't know why there is a world, why we are individuals. No matter how deeply we think and analyze, we cannot have answers to such simple questions. On top of it, we react and carry our grudges as precious belongings, protect them as if they are our children. There are no grudges in reality. We create our own joys and sorrows by our own reactions. These reactions grow within us like a small seed grows into an enormous tree. These are all aches and pains of our ego. First, it affirms itself. Then, it resents others. Next, it compels us to pass judgments on all our perceptions. This reaction creates an imagined situation of either like or dislike and becomes the story of our life. There is no pleasure or sorrow, only pure joy—not joy as created by our reaction. It is unmotivated, unconditional joy."

Radha was finally beginning to see through the layer. She was carrying a grudge against everyone she knew, giving meaning to people, events, and situations. She always felt there was a strong wall her mind hit every time she tried to think about such things. A smile crossed her lips as she realized that the mind itself was the veil.

It had begun to snow heavily. The snow blinded, yet at the same time dazzled Radha. She felt the softness of the snow embracing her, taking her in its bosom. It illuminated the space around her. All of a sudden she was filled with a wave of goodness and well-being. It had never occurred to her that she would have the opportunity to ask her unanswered questions from another face. Now it seemed to stretch to infinity—the questions and the answers becoming questions. She felt welcomed as gratitude filled her.

The woman looked at Radha in the most affectionate way and spoke, "There is a very interesting story. In a town there lived a man with two grown sons. They wanted to sell their ancestral house. It so happened, the day agreement was drawn with the buyer, a fire broke in the house. The man tried to save the house, but fire spread quickly and engulfed the whole house. The man was overcome with grief. Soon, one of his sons arrived and told him that the buyer signed the contract that morning. The father was relieved. The sadness he experienced at the loss of house was gone. In fact, he became happy. Then his other son came and told him that there was some problem and the contract did not go through. The man was devastated. It was his house getting burned. His emotions changed again."

The meaning sunk deeper into Radha as she reflected on that the central point of any experience was not the external event, but one's feeling and reaction to it. She smiled as she remembered all thoughts that went in her mind when she analyzed her feelings about her children and parents. She was right she didn't love them for their sake, but because they were her children and parents. Mist engulfing the mind was disappearing.

"The man was devastated because the relationship of ownership was there, and this apparent meaning became the source of his happiness and sorrow. The world is not the problem. The problem is our attachment or aversion to it. We either cling to it (desirable) or run away from it (undesirable). Either way, we give meaning to it. We are always affected; never remain as we are, aware and unshaken. We have to understand that these connections and meanings are just fictions, but since our mind is so caught up in fictions, it fails to recognize the fact and the fiction come alive."

The magnitude of the woman's words brought Radha to different heights of inexplicable wonder; a maze which was self-revealing. Radha went deep in thoughts and marveled at various ways a thing can be visualized. It was something in itself; it appeared to be something to the one who was beholding it; and it was related to other things. Her concept of a thing was totally independent of what the thing actually is. Imagine a mother seeing her child, full of love, and imagine a physician seeing the same child as a patient; it is the same person, but such an enormous difference in seeing. A mother cannot see what the physician sees, and the physician cannot see what the mother sees. And imagine a scientist seeing the same child through a microscope. He will not see the child but the atomic structure of a physical body. Everyone ignores such an enormous truth—that all perceptions are relational. They are not a true representation of the truth.

"We are alcoholics, drunk from the greatest alcohol of all, Ego. Truth is precedent to the action of our individualities. Though in daily life we operate through intellect and reason, it is obvious there is something in us much deeper and profounder than our intellect. We are fooled by what we see, what we are capable of seeing, and what we want to see rather than what they really are. The very existence of a thing is the basic foundation of its being. It has its own seat of consciousness." The woman was so happy that for a moment it seemed she would burst.

"It is amazing to realize whatever I see, whatever I understand, and whatever I think is forced on me and is not an act of freedom at all. I am a slave to my flawed perceptions. My loves and hatreds are practically the way in which my mind reacts to circumstances and people, due to the prejudice already in me in the form of my individuality." Radha was amazed at the answer that seemed to come out of nowhere, hiding deep inside her heart waiting for the right moment to reveal itself.

When Radha woke up the next day, she remembered vividly about her conversation with the woman. She felt a million miles away from the world inhabited by her achievements and failure, her dreams and fears. All of that seemed like a childhood memory. She felt as though she had changed into something new, and she couldn't change back. She was surprised she didn't want to change back. There was such a good feeling attached to it.

Then, she saw the woman. She was sitting on a chair across the room. Before Radha could recuperate from the dazzling effect of her presence, the woman spoke, "Just like all actors and sets are images on the screen; similarly, we are also a reflection on the screen of space. Space—Silence—is the background on which the entire world is projected, like holographic images."

"Who is projecting?" Radha asked.

"Our mind (focused consciousness) is the projector projecting various stories depending on its whim and fancy. The world is an optical illusion. We have to see it in its true form. Until the time we see forms and not the *formless*, manifest and not the *unmanifest*, we cannot know the reality of things. Reality is the *space*, space with comes from our being; the stuff you are made of and the stuff I am made of. The entire world is like an enchanting painting on a canvas. You can draw an amazing painting with minute details. No matter how beautiful or heart-capturing it is, it is still a painting. The worlds, people, stories depicted on it are still stories. What is real is the canvas, the background on which the painting is drawn. Universal consciousness is the canvas and by drawing on itself, it gets focused and manifests as various individual consciousnesses of people, trees, and different things—

ultimately, the world. To take another analogy, different shapes can be made out of clay or gold—beautiful, enchanting, and captivating things—millions and billions of them. Shapes carry intense power over our senses and mind. We get bewitched by them. We wouldn't be so enthralled if they were not made into beautiful things through creative action. In reality, there are no things but the substance out of which such infinite things are made. In the same way, there is only one consciousness. We are the background on which the world is projected! We are the thing we are searching for."

Radha felt love as she had never felt before, a caress she had never experienced, a kiss she had always longed for. She was aware of the woman's deep and loving voice resonating in her head, penetrating her mind. She saw in a flash what lay beyond, as an intimate someone without a beginning and an end; it was glorious—and then it was gone leaving a sweet remembrance. She looked at the woman, blissful.

"Imagine a statue of Buddha made of clay. How significant it becomes if Buddhist minds see it. Heads bow down in reverence automatically. Imagine a statue of Krishna from a Hindu eye. Imagine the beauty, the power, and the significance of it from that point of view. Or a statue of Jesus from a Christian eye. Now, see the same statues from an objective eye. There is no Buddha, no Krishna, and no Jesus. There is only clay. Ultimately, all things in the world are names and forms. These forms and names seem real, so real that it stirs our being in various raptures of joy and sorrow.

"We create our own experience through the persistent power of our thoughts and actions. Beauty is hidden in a lump of clay which gets revealed by the creative action of the potter. It is hidden in the mind of a painter who draws it. It is hidden in the desire of a sculptor who carves it. Even now, infinite possibilities exist as potentiality in infinite mind which will get revealed once the creative action begins. Experience is inherent in *Consciousness* just like heat is inherent in fire."

For a split second Radha forgot who or where she was. When she looked up, the woman was gone. Radha began to look for her. In another spit second she was transported to her bed. A surge of force rushed in and out of her *and* she saw it in the swiftness of her mind. It was immense and sublime—a sea of energy gushing forth in all directions, without motivation, just delight.

She knew she had experienced something extraordinary and would cherish it in the deepest chambers of her heart.

≈ 11 ≈

The Essence of Love

"I looked upon slumbering Nature, and with deep reflection discovered the reality of a vast and infinite thing—something no power could demand, influence, acquire nor riches purchase. Nor could it be effaced by the tears of time or deadened by sorrow. It is something that gathers strength with patience, grows despite obstacles, warms in winter, flourishes in spring, casts a breeze in summer, and bears fruit in autumn, I found Love"—Khalil Gibran

When Radha slept again, she found herself facing the woman. She was sitting in lotus position in the clear snow; her face had a glow that was endless. Radha was as if magnetically pulled towards her and felt that she was at the right place, that everything was well with the world.

The woman opened her eyes, and Radha asked, "You are saying all relationships are false then—relationship of parents, spouse, children, and friends?"

The woman said calmly, "Nothing is false. Everything is beautiful. Relationships are there for us to enjoy and to weep. Surrender to them. They are the most important gift of all. How would we create, express, and experience anything if there is no one to acknowledge us. Friends and foes—we need both of them. They make us come alive, make us extraordinary. But see the difference between love and relationship. Relationships are based on mutual gratification instead of love and acceptance. If someone likes me, I like that person. I respect a person for his or her talents, wisdom, and greatness. If that person stops loving me, I also stop loving, and start living in isolation and call it suffering; you judge the other. We hide behind our own pursuits and ambitions, and call it love. This is not love. When we begin to like people for what they are—for life in beating in their heart— instead of their greatness or validation, that is love. It is easy to like someone who likes you. The challenge is to like someone who doesn't like you. If you can do that, then you know the essence of love. The word has been distorted for countless ages—that it's deep essence and significance is lost on you. Relationship is not love; it is only a meaning read into a situation hanging on *ego*. If this connection is not there, there is no relationship."

What is the essence of love, then? Radha thought, like a diligent student on the verge of an amazing discovery. People have lived their whole lives in delusion, looking for perfect love, always falling to the ground, never finding it.

"Do you know what it is?" the woman asked, reading her thoughts.

"It is the mystery of all times. Everyone is looking for that magical someone called soul mate. I don't think anyone has ever found perfect love—even though it has been glorified in books and stories. I think it is a hoax. It does not exist," Radha said with an intellectual air, knowing full well that her statement was going to be contradicted.

The woman gave her a perfect smile, "Everyone is each other's soul mate. Anyone who has seen the trees, the flowers, the birds, the sun, the moon, and the stars, knows the essence of love. But we don't have the time to look at them. There is no space in our minds—so filled up with me and mine—to look at them. Nature is example of perfect love. Do you see the sun forbidding its heat and light from going to certain houses and allowing others? It does not say that whoever puffs my ego is my favorite—I will give light only to that person who worships me. No—it gives whatever it has, joyously, freely, and abundantly. This is love. Look at any tree. It gives shade and fruit to the person who takes care of it and also to that person who comes to cut it. It does not differentiate. This is love. Love is cosmic, not individual.

"Does a tree say that I love a particular leaf on a particular branch and not the others? I will give nutrition to that leaf only. Each and every leaf on each and every branch gets nourished by being part of the tree, not by doing anything else. The sun does not ask any favors in return, neither does the tree or rain. This trait is possible only in humans. We have distorted love to fit to our needs. We condemn others with our judgments and think that we are right. It is our duty to take on the task of changing others and impose our thinking on them. And we call it love. When there is acceptance, there is no relationship. Then it is just love. Whenever we expect a return for our love, it turns into a relationship.

"Love is in togetherness, not in fragmentation. It is the glue that binds everything together. Love exists in the higher whole. As individuals, we have meaning. Being part of a family, we are happier because family is a higher unit than a single person. Families become communities. Communities become country, and countries become the world. Humanity is a greater whole than a single individual. Even an individual is made of many smaller wholes—billions of cells organizing themselves into bigger wholes until the physical body is formed. Love arises whenever we become part of a greater reality, bigger than ourselves. How alive we become; how great we feel. More isolated we are, less meaning there is; joined together with others, we are more meaningful. Cells have meaning, but integrated in a body, a person arises. Drops of water are okay, but joined together make a fathomless ocean. A musical note is nice, but joined together, a symphony arises. As single individuals, we cannot do much, but together mankind is such a potent force. This wholesomeness is love."

Radha remembered when she was part of a fundraiser for tsunami victims. How surprised she was at the power a group held. There were twenty members, and they raised lot of money—it would have been impossible to collect alone. The generosity of people and the power of togetherness as a team touched her to the core. For the first time in her life she realized how powerful individuals were when they came together in a collective way for a common goal; everyone became a great force. She could feel the extraordinary depth, beauty, and significance of each and every person in her life.

"The phenomenon that organizes and integrates smaller into bigger—individuals into families, leaves into tree, parts into whole—this force is love, not the earthly love as normally understood. It is the total presence of Existence. It exists in the space connecting all. This love has been given many names. Some call this togetherness as God."

"Why can't I feel the love?" Radha asked.

"God—Love—lives in us, around us; we are surrounded by *it*. But there is no space in our minds to acknowledge love, to embrace God. Our opinions, ambitions, fear are hindering us from entering It. These fictions form an immensely strong wall whereas love dwells at the innermost point in our heart. Love is a tremendous phenomenon. It is experiencing Existence from its very center."

"How can I experience It," Radha pressed.

"The only way to experience the phenomenon of love, of God, is to transcend all mental phenomenons. We have to let go of the armor of the mind. With mind, only action and becoming is possible; Love is being. Just observe: if a stranger smiles at you, you also smile spontaneously. In that brief moment a space arises connecting you both. This space is love. You are walking and suddenly you see the sun setting beyond the horizon. You become captivated by its beauty, a delight fills you. There is no involvement of the mind. Love arises between you and the sun. It is a little throb. Whenever there is an acknowledgement without motive, love comes into existence. It is a tremendous thing. The mind is not there, only you are—the being that you are. Love happens only in that unjudged moment. An unjudged moment is a powerful moment; a beautiful moment, because it is away from the limitations of thoughts, words, and actions. It cannot be cultivated; it is a totally different phenomenon. It is the love of the formless."

Radha looked up in the sky. The whole sky opened up to her. She was back in her home, in everyday reality. There was power in trees—such beauty, depth, and strength. Each tree was magnificent and a piece of art in itself, so perfect and serene. Each branch flows into the other, adjusts itself to the other with its edges hanging out into empty space against the backdrop of the immense sky. It was breathtaking. There was so much love enveloping each and every part of the tree, it was difficult to contain it. In no time, her whole being opened up and disappeared with the trees. The trees also disappeared. What remained was love. She felt herself in creation's womb, safe and secure. It was a cocoon of joy and completeness, indestructible and fragile at the same time. There was nothing to be done, except just be.

It stopped as soon as it came. She felt the whole eternity within her. Her heart overflowed with goodness. Her mind was mesmerized with awe. Such joy and bliss! There was a kind of feeling in the whole body, almost erotic. In split of a moment, her perception changed and things went from mundane to magical. The world became magical. She looked up at the sky. The sky was looking back at her with unconditional love, winking, sharing the secret.

≈ 12 ≈

The Magic of Observation

"There is a quest that calls me, In nights when I am lone, The need to ride where the ways divide. The Known from the Unknown. And everywhere Thro' the earth and air my thought speeds, lightning-shod, It comes to a place where checking pace. It cries, "Beyond lies God!" —Carl Rice

"What can be done to avoid falling into the trap of mind? How to see the real behind the apparition, the clay behind the statue? This knowledge is good for intellectual discussion, but my mind reacts as a reflex. An image carries such a force that I see only the image. If I get angry at the image for whatever reason, I become anger. It is only later on when anger has subsided do I become aware of myself, and by then my perception is already tainted by the anger. How can this awareness of reactions be practically applied to lead a harmonious and fulfilling life?" Radha asked, full of anticipation.

She had woken up and was writing for five minutes when she was transported to some other vast place. Wherever she looked she found deep space, full of warmth and love. She was startled to see that she was in outer space without any ground to stand upon. But she did not fall. What a wonder! Suddenly fear gripped her and instantly she found herself near the sacred tree. The monk was looking at her, his eyes shining with brilliance.

Maintaining the same friendly smile, he began, "The magic words are: become a witness. Observe yourself. This is the basic alchemy: watch, observe, and witness, but without any judgment. Witness with compassion, observe with joy. No thought and reaction should escape your notice, but look at them as passing clouds. Do not interpret them. Be with the present reality, moment to moment. Slowly an amazing thing will begin to happen. You will begin to see that everything arises, remains for some time, and then passes, pleasant as well as unpleasant. You will begin to release yourself out of the reflex of reactions."

"But these reactions are embedded in me. How can observing them will release me from its clutches, and when a reaction comes, it comes with an overwhelming force," Radha tried to justify her actions.

The monk said compassionately, "When you begin to observe instead of interpreting, an astonishingly simple thing will begin to happen. You will begin to see the real. It is logic, simple and pure. Let's say you see a snake and jump to your feet. Your whole being reacts with fear. Your first reflex is to run away and hide. If at that time applying all your will-power, you choose to stay and investigate it, the real will unravel itself. You will discover that it was not a snake at all. It was a rope—that you mistook as a snake. All your fears will vanish because snake didn't exist. It was an apparition conjured up by your mind due to wrong perception. Similarly, when you start observing your reactions—resentment, anger, jealousy—you will realize their reality; they don't exist. They are the ghosts conjured up by the mind due to limited perception. All your reactions are due to your ego, but there is not a place in this entire cosmos where you will find its location because it is fictitious. It is like looking for darkness with the help of a lamp. *How can darkness exist in front of light?* How can unreality exist in front of awareness?

"When a mirage is seen on a hot day, you think water is near. With observation you know a mirage is just an illusion. There is no water. When you become a witness and observe yourself as well as the world objectively, you will still see the same world, but cease clinging to it—because now you understand that it is an illusion. It cannot quench your thirst. You will know with utmost clarity that the nectar of bliss is not outside. It is always within."

Peace descended on Radha from all directions, invisible and intangible, but stronger than anything concrete.

"When you get angry, you become the first victim of anger. You feel miserable inside, not someone else. You need to respond. In the present moment whatever the situation, respond with full awareness. Reaction comes from past experiences. Response is always spontaneous. It is only when you are without any notions that you can act spontaneously. Then, it is authentic action—because it does not depend on any prejudice or conditioning. It comes from your heart, from a depth within, pure and simple.

Radha felt light as a feather, as grace showered on her.

"Before one goes to fight in a battle, there are years of practice to make one strong and strategies are learned to help one be victorious. This is also a battle, a battle for truth. You have to understand the problem first before making an attempt to resolve it. The problem is of the mind being cluttered with too many concepts and ideas. You have to decondition everything. A mind without a thought is a divine mind and a reservoir of true knowledge. Slowly and steadily you have to make the mind pure. The path to purify the mind is observation and attention. A pure mind always remains in the present moment, for it is the only truth there is. With so many thoughts, fears, and ambitions clouding your mind, you stay in two fields only. You are either thinking of the past or imagining and planning for the future, and your past is determining your future. You have to make the mind sharp, so much that it remains in the reality as it is, not as you want it to be. Our ancestors have given the best and shortest method to do it—by observing your breath. It is the connecting bridge from the unreal to the real. Watch your breath as it comes in and as it goes out. The simplest way is to sit down quietly in solitude for some time each day and observe your breath. Then, slowly, expand this practice in whatever you are doing. Those moments where you dwell here and now are powerful moments. Instantly you will experience the truth and that will be the beginning of your quest."

Radha realized she was doing the same thing for some time. Was that the reason she was having such fountain of knowledge arising in her? *Be my own witness.*

She watched the monk walk to the corners of deep space.

Radha woke up to find herself on her bed. What an astonishing experience! Being a witness! That is what Guruji at the Ashram had advised and the woman in white suggested. *Do not identify with anything, because what is seen is not real. The real is which remains in the past, exists in the present, and will be there in the future. But there is nothing in the world which does not change. Everything is passing, transient. A newborn changes every moment as part of the phenomenon of growing up. An infant today is a toddler tomorrow, a grown up the day after, and an old person after that. It is the same person; the newborn didn't die to be replaced by a different person. An astounding change was taking place every moment—every cell in the body was dying and a new cell was being born. Everything is flowing like a river. Even this solar system will perish in the process of time. What changes is not the real. Be with the one who is witnessing the change; it is the awareness which stands above the change as the observer,* Guruji had said.

As she slept again, she found herself falling into an abyss, twirling and turning at infinite speed.

≈ 13 ≈

Ego is Perfect Expression of Love

"Your pain is the breaking of the shell that encloses your understanding. Even as the stone of the fruit must break, that its heart may stand in the Sun, so must you know pain. And could you keep your heart in wonder at the daily miracles of your life, your pain would not seem less wondrous than your joy" — *Khalil Gibran*

When she opened her eyes, Radha found herself walking in a field, a gentle breeze filling her nostrils with the fragrance of fresh earth, wet with new rain. As she walked along a sloping rise, it began to appear before her. It was splendid. There stood a magnificent castle, the sort in which the kings and queens lived. Her heart skipped a beat as she saw it. It took everything in her to remain calm. She had never seen anything like it, so royal in the vast wilderness. She walked up to the side of a staircase that led to a huge double door. The doors were unlocked and swung open easily, and she entered. She gasped. It was so stunning despite its size. Walls were covered with silk and the floors were marbled in patterns, covered in rich old rugs. The high windows dazzled the room with light.

And then, she saw the monk. He was facing the other side of the room and as he turned, the light from the window enveloped him giving him the aura of an angel.

"The ultimate deception, *Ego*, is the perfect expression of love," he said.

There was no end to the surprises. First, Ego was the ultimate deception, and now it is the perfect expression of love.

"Whose love is Ego?" Radha asked.

"It is Creation's love, love's love! It is the beginning of the universe. If we didn't have ego, we wouldn't forget ourselves and immerse into varied activities of the world and, therefore, deprive us of perfectly enriching and entertaining experiences. It is holy; otherwise, how would we express, experience and create, how would we love and live, how would we laugh and weep, how would we be joyous and compassionate. It is the *ego* of the tree that it exits as a tree; it is the *ego* of the flower that it exists as a flower. Celebrate it; otherwise, nothing would manifest. We won't exist at all."

"Enriching and entertaining experiences! Here, despair rips a heart apart and you are saying entertaining."

"What about the thrilling and elevating moments when you reach the heights of success and happiness? Why do you focus on despair and failure? Both co-exist. If you wish to touch the heights of happiness, you have to embrace the depths of despair too. Surrender to both of them. Both are different sides of the same coin, and you enjoy it, all of it. Life is full of it—the drama, the thrill, the fear, and the joy. If parents buy their child a game, would you call it a deception of parents— or an expression of their love. Sometimes games are educational, sometimes sheer joy, most of the time a mix of both.

"*Ego* is put there by Creation, out of love, so that we can experience life from different points of view. It is not an act of deception. Though *ego* does not exist in the first place but is assumed by the mind to exist in the process of creation, it is the perfect expression of love. It is like a video game where you get captivated by it and enjoy in self forgetfulness. You enjoy the adrenaline rush of simply playing the game. Either way, wining or loosing, you keep yourself entertained. Just like this beautiful, colossal castle. How enchanting it is—so lovely and captivating. But it is only an arrangement of bricks, woods, and nails brought out by the creative expression of a mind and corresponding action. It can fall, as it has risen."

"I need more elaboration to understand," Radha said.

"Who is the main character in your book?" He asked.

"Meera"

"Is she real?"

"No."

"Meera is a character created by you to express a story. What the story is about is not as important right now as the creation of the character. Creation of Meera is similar to the creation of *ego*. She is just a creation, nothing more nothing less. But, see, such an important creation. Without her, there would be no story. If there were no characters in a book, how would it progress?"

"Forget about progress, how it will even begin." Radha said excitedly, with a knowing air. This, she can understand.

"Why would you create the character of Meera? Why on Earth would you weave this web of deception, fooling others about Meera? She does not exist and you weave such an enchanting story around her, making readers fall in a web of joy and sorrow. How cunningly cruel you are!" The monk said with humor.

An insight pierced Radha and she was left startled, again.

"Now suppose, somehow, Meera assumes an identity of her own and begins to believe and, consequently, feel that she is a real person. What would the creator, in this case, you, do?"

Radha smiled, "First of all, it is not possible. Such questions wouldn't arise in her mind if I don't let them. She has no existence independent of me."

"And why would you do that, dear?" He was openly laughing now.

"To create a story. What I am trying to express demands it should be like that, to make the story interesting." As the words came out, Radha began to realize the deep significance of them.

"The world is also a story written by Creation, and people and things are different characters," the monk said simply.

"Then I am just a puppet in the hands of the unknown. It is not empowering."

"You are missing the point. There is no Meera, only Radha. There are no people and things, only the universal. You are the cosmos. If Meera starts to resent Radha for not having any freedom, this is ridiculous. Meera is the imagination of Radha. It is more like, Radha starts to identify with the role of Meera and start resenting *herself* for not giving *herself* the freedom while she is the one who is freedom. That part of Radha (the universal) which identifies with Meera (individuality) does not remember and thinks that the story (the world) she is in is real whereas she herself is the world. You are not separate but included in the universal. This is the most incomprehensible mystery of life. You are creating it—story of your life—and you are receiving everything from it," the monk said.

Radha's entire body began to vibrate with a new understanding. She fell into a deep trance. When she woke up, she found herself filled with vibrations. Her body was not physical, but tiny points vibrating at an infinite speed. There were no organs. Everything inside was hollow and empty, but that which was filled with blissful space. Goodness was caressing her and the entire world was sitting inside her. The only person she could not find was Radha. She looked everywhere from the top of the head to the bottom of the toes. There was no a place she could find herself. All was space expanding and exploding, expanding and exploding.

≈ 14 ≈

The Fallacy of Perception

"He, it is, the innermost one, who awakens my being with his deep hidden touches. He, it is, who weaves the web of this maya in evanescent hues of gold and silver, blue and green, and peep out through the folds his feet, at whose touch I forget myself. Days come and ages pass, and it is ever he who moves my heart in many a name, in many a guise, in many a rapture of joy and of sorrow." — Rabindranath Tagore

Radha watched a flock of birds flying in the sky. How do the birds know to fly in a formation in such a precise fashion without any outside help? What integrates them? The communication between them is a wonder, she thought to herself.

Her mind was getting clearer and her perception heightened. She walked down to the backyard and out the door, to the woods. Something propelled her to take a walk on her usual track. She had one blue feather in the front pocket of her sweat shirt. She came across a huge banyan tree. She recognized it. It was the same tree she had met the monk for the first time and he had walked towards her house. But it was in a dream. This was real. There was a hollow space at the bottom of the tree. She sat there and smelled the air. Pure energy was coming out of it. She let relaxation take over her, such cozy feeling.

Radha opened her eyes to find the monk sitting across her, his face inches from hers, waiting.

"Do you ever wonder how you become aware of things?" He asked without any small talk. "It takes you by surprise. How do you even know that the world exists?"

"You have asked the same question I have been wondering since the time I can remember—because I see it, I can touch it."

"The world is a perception you comprehend through your five senses, five organs of perception, and instruments of action. They are your fundamental receptive apparatus. Though on surface it appears you see through your eyes, hear through your ears, and so on—but only if your mind is working in the background. If there is a knock on the door and you are immersed in reading a book, you will not hear it."

"That's correct. Just this morning, I did not hear what Suraj was saying because I was thinking about my book and Meera. Mind precedes everything. I have heard this before."

He looked at her expectedly.

Radha thanked her stars for meeting him. She didn't want to think how. It was enough that she did.

"But where is mind? Can you see it or touch it?"

"No."

"Mind is not made of any substance present at some place; it is everywhere. It is a process rather than an entity. It is in every part of our body. That is why we are more of a mind than a physical body. We also have a huge reservoir of past impressions, habits, and beliefs which we understand as 'subconscious' and 'unconscious'. These subtle tendencies are formed due to seeing the same thing, doing the same thing over and over again. And these become our concepts and ideas. Whenever we see or understand anything, it creates a ripple in the ocean of mind. Whenever same thing happens again—after a moment or a lifetime—the ripple comes on the surface as an impression. We always use this filter of subconscious. For example, day and night follow each other. We have always seen that. We accept it as a fact, and this becomes our idea about day and night. We can do certain things and cannot do certain things"

"...like?"

"We can walk not fly. We cannot walk on water or walk through walls. We believe we are enclosed within our physical bodies since we have never experienced otherwise. Someone would call a simple phenomenon such as rain a supernatural event if one hasn't seen it before. We always operate from behind these limitations due to ages of conditioning, and they have become strong walls."

Radha was astounded. *Can she walk on water, pierce through thick wall of matter?*

"Mind is not superior to the senses. It merely organizes the information fed by the senses. You need a subtle shift in perception to see that nothing of the body, mind, and intellect is either independent or permanent. Mind sees only that which the eyes see, hears only that which the ears hear. What cannot be seen, heard, tasted, touched, or felt, cannot be known by the mind. It only has capacity to synthesize different sensations of the senses, but synthesis is not knowledge. *And* intellect is only a form of judgment passed on this organized knowledge of the mind."

Radha felt struck by lightning as some remembrances flashed in her mind. A feeling of déjà vu hit her that she was not learning such amazing knowledge but had always known. It was slumbering away in some deep corners of her heart. Something activated it. What...that she had to find out.

"We have feelings and opinions on things seen and heard only. That is why the mystery of life remains hidden," Radha muttered to herself. She knew there was more because the monk was looking at her intensely, waiting.

"How reliable are these instruments—five senses, mind, intellect, everything?" he asked in a sweet yet firm voice.

"Until a few weeks ago I believed in them, but now I am not sure," Radha answered. She stood there in a labyrinth of mysterious. As soon as she gets over one mystery, another one comes elevating her to startling new heights.

"Do the unseen and the unheard exist?" he whispered.

Radha's was intrigued.

"It is such a wonderful thing, science. It knows that whatever we see—from the vastness of the sky to the depths of the ocean, from the flow of the rivers to the grandeur of the mountains—is within the visible spectrum of light. The light seen is made up of all colors in the visible spectrum. It is just one small part of the whole electromagnetic spectrum. We don't see above and below this visible spectrum. Some animals and insects can see through infrared and ultraviolet waves. These animals and insects see different colors than us due to it. There is an astounding invisible universe we fail to see."

Radha nodded in agreement.

"We are surrounded by electromagnetic fields, radio waves, gamma waves and so on. We are not aware of them, but they exist nevertheless. There are various elaborate equipments available now, highly technician cameras and monitors through which we can see infrared lights and hear subtler sounds. A different world becomes visible. Even right now where we are standing if seen through these sophisticated cameras, we may see a totally different view. Till the time science was not able to find them, we didn't know.

"What we see, we assume to be real. Even our science is based on the assumption that everything is real. We see a tree in front of us. We touch it. There is a sensation at touch. The tree becomes real. This is a dangerous definition, but we cannot have any other definition."

"I doubt if anything is real, after what has been happening to me," Radha said in mirth. In her mind, Radha bowed her head in sacred reverence.

"The reason behind seeing a shape and so forth is due to the fact that the structure and constitution of our mind is on the same level as the structure and constitution of the world we perceive. We cannot hear music if radio is not switched on, or when a different frequency is on. The music is still going on all the time. There are so many channels on television. We can see and hear only one at a time since our senses are not as subtle as the wavelengths of electrical messages emitted by broadcasting stations. There exist countless other worlds in the small space between you and me. But the density and constitutions of such worlds are subtler than the constitution of our present individuality."

An understanding was beginning to take hold that she could hear and see the monk because the frequency of her senses was getting attuned to the frequency of his senses.

He looked at her as if he knew what was going on in her mind. "A world need not be real merely because we see it. It only shows we are led to believe by our senses that this is all there, which are flawed to begin with. We are on the same level of reality as the atmosphere around us. Universe is made more of unseen, unheard, and unimaginable things than one can even conceive of. There is a mystery hidden behind to be unraveled.

"Multiple other dimensions exist, but we don't recognize them. All of us have felt these dimensions at one time or another; in moments of breathtaking beauty, endless ecstasy, or deep sadness when everything seems to stop. Whatever is observed through our senses is conditioned by the nature of the senses, like lenses. Every human being sees like a human. If we have x-ray eyes or microscopic vision, we will see a different world altogether. And yet we cannot say it would be a wrong perception."A mischievous smile spread on his face as he played with her mind.

Radha took a deep breath. "This is monumental. Just like Alice in Wonderland."

"Yes, just like Alice in Wonderland. We live amidst the magical, but, sadly, never recognize it, don't even wish to see beyond the strong wall of our perceptions. Difference between Alice and us is that she knew she was in wonderland. We live in wonderland but not acknowledge it. When we look at a tree, we see its visible part. It is not the whole picture. An extensive, elaborate system of roots remains hidden from our view. If we look at the same tree under a microscope, we see molecules, atoms, vibrations, and ultimately energy. The fact that there can be another way of thinking is either a wonder or something incomprehensible. We have to be open to the fact that there are many aspects to the universe which our senses cannot even begin to grasp. If they did, we would see many more things in this intelligent and beautiful universe."

May be she got more senses now! Radha thought about all the things she was experiencing—the expansion of space and the feeling of thrill. She wanted to ask the monk but something in his voice stopped her. It was almost a whisper. She tried hard to make out the words but his voice kept going further away from her.

Then, it was darkness and silence.

It was three o'clock, and everything around her stood perfectly still. The wind had died but the day was cold. She moved her foot and looked down. The grass under her feet turned green as she watched. It kept on growing green until the whole patch where she stood turned lush and green, glowing in the golden light. She smelled roses and jasmine and marigolds, their yellow and orange heads gently swaying with the rest. The roses bloomed, red and yellow, purple and pink, and the air grew fragrant with their perfume. Fragrance was coming from inside her as well as from inside the flowers. It was one and the same place, a depth within.

She swept out her hand over the jasmine, filling the air with magic and delight. Many other flowers of various colors and shapes shot up, yellow, white, shades of pink and red. She stood still. There was no sound, not even the shifting of the wind. She had never seen anything so beautiful. The garden filled her with the joy of beauty, of everything that was throbbing with life. It took her breath away. It had come from nothing. It grew wherever she turned her gaze.

Submerged in the beauty and joy of life, she stood there oblivious of the movement of time. The day turned into evening, light shifted from golden to pale yellow, but the flowers seemed to glow more as the light faded as though each petal was illuminated from within. It was a beauty she could not capture with imagination. Each bloom was a perfect piece of the immense.

"Radha"

She heard her name and turned towards the voice.

The monk was standing amidst the splendid brilliance of the garden. His face was lit up by brilliance too, a masterpiece of kindness and compassion.

He said, "If you were a fish, you would see, hear, and feel fish things. Your perception would be limited to that world only. To a fish, the ocean is the world. To a snail, the universe is a big line which it covers in a day. It may just be a distance of hundred steps. We know the world is big but not that snail, because its perception is limited to its structure. There is enormous difference between the psychology of a human and of an animal and also between different animals. This difference profoundly affects the perception of the physical world by each being."

Radha was forced to think in a profound way. A whole new world was opening before her.

"If you look at a building and a fish looks at it, and also an ant and a snail, everyone will see different things. Snail may not even feel the building exists. It won't recognize and, therefore, acknowledge its presence. If it did, it would look at it as something frightening, because it does not understand the objects of the world as they exist for us. Our most ordinary concepts and its richness would be completely mysterious to the snail's mind and to other beings inhabiting one or two dimensional space (insects, bugs, different animals, and so on). They need to cease to be lower dimensional being and evolve to human dimension if they wish to have even a little bit of human world's knowledge."

There was a strange look in his eyes as he spoke further, "Two subjects, living in the same world will inhabit different worlds, due to differences in their structure of senses. They cannot know one another as they really are but as they perceive each other through their knowing faculty. There are thousands and thousands of level of perception existing parallely in the same world. Because we are humans, we have human perception and not some other. Even two human beings, different members of the same family, live in totally different worlds due to difference in their perception of the world."

"Even two different human beings..."

"Yes. Ask any two siblings. Given the same environment and subject to the same rules, care, and love, they would have different perceptions of their parents and believe that nothing happened in quite the same way. If perceptional faculty worked at the same level in all humans, they should see no such difference in their experiences. Our perceptional faculty is influenced by the way we relate to the world. Remember, a mother sees her child and a physician sees the same child differently. Observe any street in any city or town; you will invariably see people going on their way, living in their minds, totally oblivious to the things happening around them in reality."

He continued further, "Just like lower dimensional beings either observe our three dimensional world with wonder or are not even aware of it, we are also not aware of the world as it is but as we perceive it through our sense perceptions. Nothing real can be known through the relative activities of the senses since they change according to the spatial temporal structure within which they function. As humans, we receive incorrect impressions of the world. In the very act of receptivity, the world is distorted in our eye. And we know it is distorted. It is not as it appears."

"We know it is distorted!" Radha said.

"When we see distant objects as dots, since our sight is not equipped to see at such long distances. We know something is there but don't know what it is until it comes closer. When we mistake a certain thing for something else entirely, like mistaking a small tree in the night as the shadow of a stranger lurking in the darkness. In a study of a person blind by birth, it was noted that for some days after his sight was regained medically, he did not recognize what he saw. People and things appeared to him as moving lights and shadows even though his sight was restored completely. It was only after he was trained to look, could he begin to understand and see things. Other instances are when we submerge our hands in freezing water and right after in hot water, it takes some time for senses to register the burning sensation. If some physical pain is there, medication eases it. If the pain is real, medicine should not affect it."

Radha saw a bug on the ground, but as she stared at it, it turned out it was just a twig.

The monk smiled, "Once upon a time, there came on this earth a great scientific mind who was baffled by the working of the universe. So he decided to observe it. He observed that if we are sitting inside a moving train, and another train comes on parallel tracks and is moving at a different speed, we would have the illusion of the trains moving at much different speeds than they really are."

So many times Radha wished she had met and known scientists of all times. Science and art both looks at the world in the same way, with wonder. Each chose to express it in different ways, one with scientific experiments and theory, and another with poetry, words, and paintings, both equally great expressions.

The monk continued, "There is another common occurrence. I call it *the phenomenon of fan*. When a fan moves at a high speed, it seems not to be moving at all. Speed gives it an appearance of solidity. There are many more illusions which we see and believe but on closer scrutiny realize the structure and mystery behind them."

"Are you saying what I think you are saying? If this is correct, then it is not just a wonder but the most frightening thing I have ever heard. It threatens to consume my mind with its implications. The world as I see is not the property of the world but the property of my receptivity to the world!" Radha gasped. The strength in her legs gave away, and she had to sit down on the ground. She was feeling giddy.

"What I am going to say next might slip from the grasp of your mind. It is not a fantasy. We see the world as we see it because it is reflected in our consciousness as such. If we know there is receptivity lower than ours, it also proves the possibility of higher receptivity than ours. There may be some community of beings, living side by side, on higher receptivity than ours whom we cannot see because we don't comprehend them. Perhaps, they are looking at us this very moment like we look at the snail."

Radha jumped to her feet and looked all around herself to see if someone was watching them. Her mind was in a maze of wonder, holy wonder.

She smiled and the monk smiled with her, as if he could see the beings on higher plane.

"This is sensational...and bizarre."

"And when we transcend to that higher receptivity and that is, if, then, we will see and understand that the world, as we perceive it now, does not really exist, has never existed. It is as real as the stillness of a moving fan, the water in a mirage, the illusion in motion."

"I always felt something was wrong at the way I look at things, but never in my wildest dreams did I imagine that my whole perception of the world could be so distorted," Radha bursted out.

Something inside her stirred and a new vision began to take shape. In a flash, Radha found herself back in her room. *The world is not real just because we can see it* was her last thought as she drifted to sleep that night.

≈ 15 ≈

The Original Lie

"Not to be held bondage to cold and heat, not to be ripped apart from love and hate; from desire and fear; from success and failure is freedom."

The following morning she woke up with a sharp pain in her right leg. She had cut herself the previous night as she was walking in the garden a sharp branch had pierced her skin. She looked at it in wonder. How was it possible? It was a dream. How could she cut herself in a dream and have the wound transferred to the waking life? Unless it did! She looked at her usual worldly possessions and saw them fade away, as in a dream. She felt guilty on making them unreal, but she could not negate the presence of something higher and beyond—which she had experienced first as an external something and then within herself. All her life, her beliefs, her culture, her education defined her; they limited her. Now when the mind had quieted down, right knowledge had come to illumine the light within. So much love and compassion exists in the unknown, but the mind dwells on the fear of losing the known, not knowing that the known was contained in the unknown. By diving into the ocean of the unknown, one doesn't lose the known but creates it.

Radha went for her usual morning walk. She saw another blue feather on the ground. She was holding it when it happened again. She was on the snow clad mountain, and the woman with angelic face was walking towards her.

The woman's sweet voice rendered her powerless. "We believe that the world is a container holding us, just as water is contained in a pitcher with no connection between the two. We believe we are separate from the world."

"Is it not the truth?" Radha gasped, and then took a deep breath knowing she was on the brink of eternity.

"What is meant by outsideness?" The woman asked.

"Outside means outside; I can look at it as outside me." Radha was puzzled by her line of questioning. First, the world was not real, and then not external. There was no end to the marvel called creation.

"Apply the mind and see through the elegance of seduction. There are always three parts to an experience—a subject, an object, and the act of perception. The object is what is seen or experienced. The subject is the seer or the experiencer. In my context, whatever is 'not me' is the object—in this case, the world. Whoever perceives it as outside is the subject—in this case, me. An object could be anything conceivable in space and time as external and separate from the subject from its point of view. Whatever is not the subject is outside. And this becomes the content of my consciousness. This consciousness of externality is the world. Do you understand. This is a profound point," the woman said delightfully. Everything about her was delightful.

"'Outside' is not the trees, the people, the planets, or the stars. It is an externality, a separation of things from each other!" Suddenly Radha felt excitement rising within.

The woman said, "There is something very intriguing about the subject (me), and objects (the world). Objects are an appearance of the very same thing of which I am also an appearance. Both are hanging on each other for their subsistence. If outside does not exist, there is no inside and vice versa. The whole problem is of externality. The world is a space-time complex. Think deeply and see if there was no space-time, there would be no externality of perception and, therefore, no world-experience. We would not see each other. We would be at the same place, or rather, merge with each other."

"But it is impossible to know things except in space-time," Radha said. For a moment she felt she transcended space-time and had become the embodiment of all things. There was no outside. The entire world was existing within her, as her. She held her breath longer than usual, without knowing. As she let go of the breath, a strange feeling came over her, joy and warmth began to flow in and out of her.

"Space-time complex is a type of make believe. We believe, firmly and sincerely, the world to be a vast space in which we exist as fishes exist in the ocean. A fish cannot become the ocean, and water cannot become the fish. The world cannot become me, and I cannot become the world. But there is a monumental connection between the vast space-time complex and physical matter, between the world and individuals, between the mind and physical body. Matter is formed or, rather, energy is crystallized into varied physical forms due to its mystical involvement with space-time complex, including our own bodies. We don't recognize the mysterious connection because we are also involved in this process of crystallization.

"Albert Einstein was the first one to find out scientifically that matter is energy in motion. Space-time and matter are not independent of each other, but form one whole as the fabric of the cosmos. I remember now," Radha marveled at such a staggering discovery the world was given and yet life went on as usual.

"Long before him, the ancient seers not only found out but also experienced the truth in their deep acts of meditation. Is the world really an object?" the woman further asked Radha.

"Well, I can see it as an object. On a second thought, I am also a part of it, looking at it like an object," Radha was surprised at her own answer. She had not thought about herself and the world like that. But then, no one had asked her that question. She was bewildered at the knowledge buried deep within her. Now, with right questions it was surfacing.

"Glaciers and icebergs are parts of the ocean that have solidified into ice, but they are not really separate from the ocean. Though a distinction can be made between the ice and water, it is the same continuum. Same is the connection between the world and the individual, between the divine and human. There is no distinction between the astronomical solid reality of the universe on one hand and so-called empty space on the other, no distinction between you and me whatsoever," the woman said excitedly, like a scientist on the brink of a discovery. "This is the most vital truth. The world is external to me is an *original lie* on which Creation stands. The world and I are as insepara- ble as two waves in the ocean."

Radha was transported to eternity. For a moment, she had no con- sciousness of what was happening and was just aware of her presence in the space inside her.

The woman spoke, "The world is not really outside, that is the point. Everything is included within itself. We are the icebergs and glaciers in the ocean. The difference between God, world, and human is the same difference that exists between vapor, water, and ice."

The woman paused for a moment, joy radiating from her in all di- rections.

"Let's take your physical body. Your finger is part of your body. If somehow the finger gets a consciousness of its own, something like an individual ego, it would think itself to be an independent entity. But the finger cannot function on its own independent of you. They form one organic whole. Merely looking at things cannot be regarded as a proof of their externality. The entire cosmos is one organic organism. Just because you can look at it as external to you, does not mean it is really outside you."

"This is more bizarre than the mind can ever imagine."Radha glanced at her fingers and the space around.

The woman said, "Science has also confirmed the truth of every- thing in space and time being connected to everything else. It is a fact that every cell in our brain is organically connected to every atom in the cosmos. We have the entire cosmos within. We are enveloped by a mystery we cannot solve; we are a marvel we cannot comprehend, an impulse we cannot describe. There is a splendor to our being that can- not be articulated. It can only be experienced at and as the foundation of our being."

An understanding began to take hold in Radha's heart. She was still immersed deep in thoughts when she reached the backyard. She re- membered walking on the trail leading to the house, but after that she got lost in the maze of her mind. She glanced at her watch. Her heart skipped a beat as the realization dawned on her that it was still 8 in the morning, the exact time she had left for the walk! Radha forced herself to think hard. Surely she hadn't entered another dimension which had no time. It was the trail she walked every day for the past year. How was it possible to have such a long conversation with someone without any time passing? Unless, it did stop!

Radha would have walked straight if she hadn't noticed a small stone glittering in the afternoon sun. She looked at it. There was something odd about it. She gasped as she realized it was breathing! Before she could react, another blue feather similar to the one she had was sticking out of it, also breathing. Small whisper like breaths, in perfect alignment with her own breaths! She was still looking at it in curiosity when the angelic woman in white came walking towards her. Radha had long stopped racking her brain for logical answers. Nothing in her life had remained logical.

The woman continued the conversation they were having earlier. Radha felt a warmth surge throughout her body, as if her body were a lamp shade illuminating everything around. Slowly, the glow spread outward, embracing everything that came in its path, filling everything with brilliance.

"The fact that we are individuals cannot be regarded as the ultimate truth; being an individual is a phenomenon. Our individualities, our desires and fears, our relationship with people and things are certain conditions we are passing through temporarily in the process of evolution. The so-called physicality of our body can lose its substantiality anytime. It is only a concept, to which we cling so much. We are the condensation of cosmic stuff and can be reduced to ethereal substance."

Radha was on the verge of becoming ethereal herself. She wasn't sure what was happening and didn't care either. It was such a warm feeling to be disturbed with a thought.

"Still, we remain within the realm of thoughts and find comfort in the idea that we are independent and can stand on our own. It is a big illusion. Certain forces have combined in a particular shape for certain purposes, under certain conditions; it is beyond human comprehension, or imagination. Our true identity is not with the infinite relationships with things and people. Our true identity is with the entire cosmos—for we are the cosmos."

Radha tried to think, to bring any thought to the surface, but her mind refused to yield. She stood there suspended, without the slightest movement in the mind. Instantly she felt the whole humanity standing next to her. Everyone who had ever lived was there—or rather, existed at the same point in space and time at which she existed! They were aware of her, and now she was aware of them. They existed in her. She existed in them. How frightening! She feared death had come to claim her.

A flood of relief rushed over as thoughts came rushing back in. Now she could live as the feeling of death receded in the background, but not before her mind shook with the strange, astounding knowledge.

The woman was looking at her, with an affectionate smile. "Just think how you know that another being exists."

"How?" Never did she think about such a question.

"I am here, you are there. An intelligible medium has to exist between us, which, at the same time is also standing above us—so that we can have the knowledge of each other."

"That's logical."

"But there is nothing, practically, between us, except empty space." The sun shone brightly behind the woman and its brilliance blinded Radha for a split second as the woman tilted her head slightly.

"Yes, this is a strange phenomenon," Radha said inquisitively.

"If our perceptions are due to our mind and senses, then they have to touch the objects to be aware of their presence. Then, we have to touch each other to be aware of each other's existence. A mind is not even physical, whereas objects are physical. How can we reconcile this great distinction in their essentiality?"

"That's not possible. My mind has to touch the sun and stars, which are several light years away," Radha objected. It was ridiculous. Then her body should also travel to the stars in a flash. Such a thing has never been heard of.

"Think. Be a scientist. Like a detective, go to the end or to the beginning of the mystery. Latest scientific discoveries are saying that parallel lines can meet under certain circumstances if stretched through infinity, and concepts of physical laws may not hold well in subatomic realms. We have to be open to the fact that deeper truths than the mind thinks may exist. Otherwise, great discoveries in the field of science and, also, in spirituality cannot be comprehended. It is only when the mind is open to the impossible, that it can reach the truth."

"I give up," Radha said after a long pause.

The woman looked at her intensely, "An undercurrent of *consciousness* is necessary for any perception. We have to have some sort of *consciousness*. We cannot be inert. The existence of objects also proves the presence of *consciousness*, since existence and *consciousness* go together."

"We are taught letters and numbers in school but not this. This is fundamental and frightening at the same time," Radha said.

"Whenever there is a perception of an object by the observer, there is a connection of *consciousness* between the observer and the observed. The act of experience itself is repudiation of the notion that subjects are cut off from the objects, that I am cut off from you. If there were a gulf between the subjective consciousness and objective reality, then there would be no such thing as experience at all."

Radha felt she had entered a science class, a very illuminating science class. "The world is not independent of consciousness! It is the glue which holds this structure in place—me, you and everything in between. I see, I hear, I smell, I touch, I think, I feel, the whole nine yards—the magic of my being, within and without! It is always here and now, and everywhere. I exist in it, I am of it and still unable to grasp it. Why don't I see this undercurrent of consciousness?" Radha questioned.

"That which exists within space is not an object of perception. Since our senses are not equipped to grasp the subtlest of the subtler, we completely ignore the invisible and intangible. As in a circus, we watch acrobats doing incredible stuff. A man is standing and suddenly he is flying in mid air. We become so mesmerized by such great performance that we fail to see he is flying in the air suspended on an almost invisible rope. Similarly, we are so enchanted by this incredible world that we fail to see almost invisible undercurrent of consciousness, gluing us together in this wonderful performance of the world."

"If I shift my eyes a little bit, I can see the rope," humored Radha.

"That's right. And that's all that is needed, just a slight shifting of the mind to see through the deception, to undo the spell," she said.

Radha marveled at the play of consciousness; her heart was filled with gratitude and reverence for the universal. She was gradually getting illumined with pure knowledge. Her heart was racing at an infinite speed.

"Everything in the world has pure subjectivity in itself. The objective reality is *also* the subjective consciousness. From my point of view I am the subject and you are the object, but when you perceive me then I am the object and you are the subject. If I am the subject to myself, you are the subject to yourself, and everyone and everything is a subject from its own point of view, then the objects don't exist. It is only a facade. The entire objective reality is inhabited by the subjective consciousness."

"Please explain more," Radha said.

"One can be an object from another's points of view, but from its own point of view, it will always be the subject. From the giant mountains to the minutest atoms, this subjectivity is present in every little nook and cranny of the creation. I know you as 'I', and you also know me as 'I'. There is nothing outside this intriguing 'I', which begins within our hearts and spreads beyond any imagination. Illusion arises because we see only a part and not the whole. A transcendental presence connects us to the world, creating such breathtaking universe of interrelated particulars, like waves in the ocean. It is only a point of view that is called the subject; it is also only a point of view that is called an object. If all points of view are lifted to the universal point of view, there would be neither subjects nor objects but one whole indivisible existence. Just like various colors are reflected from white light or separate cups are filled from one pot of tea—the basic essence of all is same. There is only one being. It is called *consciousness*—aware of its existence."

A powerful emotion had risen in Radha, threatening to smash her mind to the ground. She remembered nothing. She forgot nothing. She stood still, absorbing the knowledge pouring on her.

A snail was walking on the ground. It appeared to hardly move. It seemed the time had stopped and all existence was contained in one snail. The snail had consciousness of its own. It looked at the whole world, with Radha and the woman, as objects. How the mind, self-possessed by arrogance, fails to see this bewildering fact and treat the world as an object, whereas in reality it is as much a subject as her, Radha marveled.

The woman whispered, "The observer does not stand apart from the observed or the act of observation, but they form a single organism of a thing grand. Due to cosmic mystery, this vital connection is not grasped. Mind cannot capture its essence because it works in time. If this interconnection can somehow be acknowledged and embraced, then there would be an immediate merger of all into a single ocean of being, throbbing and intelligent being, exploding with bliss every moment, eternally. It is called a glimpse. From there on our real journey begins."

Radha felt a chill went down her spine. There were electric like vibrations flowing through her.

It had begun to drizzle, small droplets of water were pouring from the sky. Radha let a feeling of well-being envelope her like a blanket, with tears of joy rolling down her cheeks. She wanted to stand there forever and be immersed in the glory of existence.

≈ 16 ≈

The Wonder of Knowledge

"I dive down into the depth of the ocean of forms, hoping to gain the perfect pearl of the formless." —Rabindranath Tagore

When she woke up at some time in the night, she remembered every-thing: about the snail, the fish, and everyone inhabiting different per-ceptions; the world not being real, but reflected as such in conscious-ness through different perceptional apparatus. What kind of wonder is this—the world. How can such a thing be? No matter which way she took, her mind brought her to amazing heights of wonder. She reached a zero point where she stood suspended on nothing. There was nothing her mind could do; it had become redundant as anything.

The moonlight shone through the window. Suraj slept besides her, his slow breathing filling the air with the sweetness of familiarity and the known. It was a relief, to see him.

It was no use. She sat up and put her feet on the floor. Her body shivered with the cold. Still delight filled her. She switched open the lamp on the side of the bed. Light filled the room instantly, almost blinding her. She looked around: two chairs in the far corner of the room, a dresser right in front of the bed. Everything was as she re-membered. She turned off the light. Instantly, moonlight flooded the room, illuminating everything within the room as well as within her heart.

What beauty! Such magnificence! She marveled at how could the brilliance of beauty be hidden by one tiny bulb? The moon was so big, its brilliance covered the limitless sky, but she couldn't see it. A tiny dot of light bulb could hide the dazzling beauty of the moon. A tiny dot of her mind and ego—of ignorance—could hide knowledge, so vast and immeasurable.

Radha stood at the edge of the cliff of a mountain. The view from there was staggering. The mountains were magnificent against the backdrop of the immense sky. They stood with open arms, welcoming creation in its embrace. She also stood there, rooted and enchanted at their splendor. In the morning, she took her usual trail, but somewhere in middle she took a different turn and found herself face to face with eternity. It took her breath away. She gasped, and then waited for the racing heart to come to normal. She wanted to merge with silence and the beauty, become one with it. She had an impulse to jump. Hypnotizing existence was welcoming her with open arms.

And she jumped without any fear, only thrill.

She was not surprised to realize she was not falling. The creation had taken her in its bosom, playing with her as a mother plays with her child. She moved freely, climbing hills and mountains as she played in her backyard. It was not some miracle but the most natural thing. It was not a dream either. She was fully awake and conscious of what was happening, remembered all her adventures in different dimensions. She pinched herself to be sure and realized she was moving without a body! It seemed she had left her body at some point in space and time, and was now spread everywhere without a beginning and an end. What was happening didn't seem to be clear, but she didn't care either. It was the most joyous and intoxicating feeling—of total abandon and freedom without any limitations.

After a while, she felt being sucked into a whirlpool of space, retaining her consciousness at all times. She wasn't crushed to death since there was no physical body to be crushed. The whirlpool was also her. She was moving within herself in a way which defies any logical explanation. With some twists and turns at an infinite speed, like a ride in an amusement park, she found herself in deep space with stars forming and bursting around her. The deep space was full of Silence; Silence that was breathing, conscious, and scintillating with awareness.

It was welcoming as she breathed it, walked with it, and finally, became one with it. She became aware of a tingling sensation beginning to form in her legs and slowly spreading upwards towards her head.

It was her last remembrance before she fell into a sweet sleep. She woke up to find herself in her bed and glanced at the clock on the right wall of the room. It said two o' clock. Suraj was deep asleep, and everything was still and quiet. Only thing she could hear was her own breathing.

Radha knew she hadn't dreamt the whole thing, from her walk in the woods to her trip to the space. A mind as finite as hers cannot conjure up things so infinite in nature. Such feelings of completeness, of bliss—she had never known those feelings before. It wasn't a dream either. It was a fact. She slept again with a conviction that all was well with the world.

After an hour, she felt something was going to happen, like a sneeze coming, and in a flash found herself inside the hollow of the sacred tree. It was just as she begins to experience a dream. She does not know how she gets there. But she was not dreaming. That was the point. It was as if her mind froze and someone brought her there, and then thawed her mind and senses.

There was half a foot of space between her and the inside of the tree. She got up and took a step towards her left. The space inside the tree also expanded. She took a step towards her right. The same thing happened. Had she stumbled on a hidden path, she wondered. She began to walk. To her astonishment, wherever she walked the space expanded endlessly.

She felt a stirring. The monk was coming towards her from inside the space.

He began to speak as soon as she saw him, "The correct perception is seeing everything in its original form. It is seeing the energy hidden behind matter, lost in the bliss of existence. It is entering Reality from its center. It is love."

Radha tried to speak but nothing came out of her mouth.

He spoke further, "We think that the physical world is the only reality. It may be a mountain, a chair, or a living body—that makes no difference—everything is physical. But as we observe closer, in labs and under highly technical microscopes, physical elements recede from our view and in their place come molecules, atoms, electrical charges, and eventually energy vibrating at an infinite speed. And energy is not spatial; it is everywhere. It is beauty. It is intelligence. It is joy. It is me. It is you. It is every blessed thing. It exists at each and every point in space and time. As it vibrates in a particular manner, it is perceived as an object, as me and you. In reality, the object is not there, I am not there, you are not there at all. It is all a holographic image."

Radha couldn't help but touched her face to confirm she was there.

"We are surrounded by millions and billions of things, but they are various dimensions of one single thing. The entire universe is a single continuum of joy. It is moving at such a high speed that it gives an apparition of stable solidity. The hardest rock is only a bundle of intense vibrations. Since we are profoundly seduced with the spell of distorted perception, we fail to perceive the underlying essence. We have separated ourselves from others. This is called Creation. See it this way. Everything in Cosmos can be reduced to its elements, whatever is its character. The ice is made up of water, so is the snowflake or vapor. Though their function and purpose is different, their character is water. The knowledge of water also implies the knowledge of the ice, the snowflake, the vapor, and all things made of water. Applying the same principle to everything in the universe, we come to the conclusion that everything is made of a single substance! Science calls it energy, humans call it God."

"Energy is God?" gasped Radha.

"Energy not as science describes it, but energy which is intelligent and conscious—*the thing in itself*—which science has not been able to understand, not yet. The universe is not created. Because if it is created then there can be no evolution. It reduces the entire creation to a thing including human consciousness."

"But everything is changing and evolving," Radha said.

There was a knowing smile on his face as he continued, "Yes, evolution means creation continues; it is endless. We may believe that God is a super person sitting in heaven, passing judgments, but the facts of nature tell a different story. God is life. *And* life is intelligent, always reaching new possibilities and heights, always evolving to a better stage."

He paused for a moment before proceeding further, "If we go by the rules of logic as a means to acquire knowledge, it is basically classification. Aristotle is known as the father of logic and was the first one, who in his ceaseless endeavor to attain knowledge began to group and classify—from plants to animals, from ocean to land, from earth to sky, and everything in between. The rules of logic state that all particulars are explained through generalities. Finding the *unity in variety* is knowledge in the present context."

"Aristotle was a disciple of Plato. I remember reading about him," Radha said.

"We have a need to know everything and whenever we find something new, we instantly move towards finding common factors with other known things. Extraordinary and unexplained facts disturb our minds, but as soon as an explanation is found, they cease to disturb, and the thing is considered known. Just because something is put into a category and a classification is made, it becomes ordinary, whereas the unknown remains extraordinary. It does not mean that the ordinary experiences of our lives, such as walking, eating, and breathing are less magnificent than the magical. There is nothing ordinary about a heart beating on its own or the food digesting in our bodies or the lungs breathing continuously from the beginning to the end."

"Ordinary satisfies, extraordinary startles, I have heard it before."

"Here is a simple truth if your mind is ready to sit and listen. Applying the same rule of finding the *unity among variety*, everything in this cosmos—living or non living, material or non-material—comes under the ultimate category, *Existence*. Everything exists. If something does not exist, its absence exists. It is the highest generalization. I exist, you exist, and this universe exists. We have made the fiction alive and living fiction by believing otherwise. Existence is eternal. In that sense God is eternal, for God is Existence. God is an intelligent presence where everything is functioning in greatest harmony—the trees, the bugs, the birds, the people, and the rivers, the mountains, the glaciers, and the earth, the stars, the moon; everything together. This wholeness is God. It is the cohesive force in the universe, binding a mother to the

child, an individual to the family, and families to the world. If we analyze and dissect this phenomenon, we can never find God. Just like if
we dissects a man, we can never find the presence that is making him
alive, the presence that is called love, the intelligent throbbing consciousness."

"There, still, exist some doubts in my mind about your theory."
Radha said.

"It is not a theory. It can be experienced as the essential truth at the
foundation of everything. You are an expression of creation. You know
you are a person. To be more specific, a being, because you feel and
think, you are conscious of your existence. This is the innermost truth
of which you are made of. No one tells you that you exist, and you
don't stop existing because somebody says you don't exist no matter
how powerful, how respected, or how intelligent that someone is. It is
experiential, not intellectual. You know that others are also conscious
because you interact with them; they behave in a similar way. As for
other things of the world, like a rock, normally assumed to be dead
matter— it has refused to stay dead and sprung to life as moving vibrations when observed under powerful microscopes. And Life is where
the movement is. There is nothing dead in the universe—everything is
pulsating with life and throbbing with joy. It is a friendliness. God is
only a name we have given to the Consciousness inhabiting the world.
This is the supreme truth. When you go inside yourself, then you will
know the truth without a doubt, just like there is no doubt in your
mind of your existence. This is the only tribute you can give to the divine."

"This is too much. I want to die. Objects are hard, I can touch them,"
Radha picked up a stone and hurled it onto her left foot. "It hurts. How
can you say that everything is a continuum of energy, so that there is
no distinction between myself and any other thing. Then I am this
world. Though highly flattering, it is totally preposterous. Look, this is
me, and this is a stone. That is the sky, and that is you. There are boundaries. We know there are these boundaries."

"What boundaries?" the monk asked patiently.

"Boundaries of physicality; if I pinch myself, I feel pain, not someone else."

"Is it so? If your child gets hurt, you don't feel any pain?"

"That is different."

"It is all the same. You feel pain because you identify with your child. You feel physical pain if something happens to your body because you identify with it."

"I identify with it because I am born with it," Radha felt the stupidity of her own words.

"You said it. You are born with it. You are not it. You have a body. You are not the body. Boundaries are illusionary. You build four walls enclosing space and call it a room. The space in different rooms is not different, notwithstanding the boundaries created. We are intensely intoxicated with the alcohol of *ego*. It hinders us from seeing the real conditions of the objects. "

A gentle breeze was flowing, giving Radha delight. She saw a tree and before a thought could capture her mind, she found herself spread in its roots, spreading upwards to various branches of the tree. She opened her eyes. She was lying on the bed, allowing the sweetness and warmth of freedom to take her to different heights. She closed her eyes and again found herself spread in the magnificence of the tree. Feeling exhilarated, she hugged Suraj sleeping beside her with all her might. She didn't want to wake up, not just yet.

"We are aware of space, we know time, and we observe something coming from something else in the cause-effect relationship. Can there be knowledge without objects or thinking without space?" the woman asked, carrying the simple expression of motherly love. She had appeared when Radha was enjoying her freedom away from the limitations of her body.

"Is there...?" Radha was still smiling from the effects of being a tree. The distinction of the two things at two different points in space had vanished that morning as she had entered the being of the tree. Or maybe it was the tree which had entered her being—she may never know.

"We have to give up the three dimensional thinking and enter into a higher dimension. This dimension is wonderful as well as frightening since it breaks our usual way of thinking. Here, logic ceases to work and all beliefs are smashed to the ground. How can we see a simple process of one thing becoming another—when energy is generated through motion or when a caterpillar transforms into the butterflies— and still not be mesmerized."

"Why is it so elusive?"

"Can your fictional character Meera know her creator? Meera cannot know Radha as an object because she is part of Radha. Total inclusiveness cannot become the object of our perception. What we have is the information—length, breadth, colors—not an insight into the nature of things. If I know you birth date, height, weight, color, country, and religion—that does not mean I know you. Even knowing you intimately is not to know you. Different people know you differently depending on the relationship that exists between you and them. To know you truly, I have to become you. Our knowledge of things is already tainted by our opinions and prejudices. This is the action of our senses, not knowledge. It is right from our point of view, but not from the point of view of reality as such. To know the universe truly, we have to transcend it. We have to transcend our mind, and we have to transcend space and time."

That was the last the woman said before disappearing into the thin air. Radha sat down to collect her thoughts when 'the feeling' came as a flash, and then it was gone. In its place came the endless chatter from the mind. But for that one flash of the moment she experienced that she, the walls, and the furniture in the room were part of the same continuum. She merged with them; there was no beginning and no end to her being. In deep meditation where no thought could reach, true knowledge came in flashes and shook the very foundation of the mind she was standing on. She realized that she and the cosmos were not two independent entities standing apart as the perceiver and the perceived but, together, they formed a complete organism of an indivisible grandeur.

Meera
Written By: Radha

≈ 1 ≈

Meera

"I have been standing on the seashore, and whatever I have gathered is sand in my fist, nothing more. And this is a great, infinite expanse. Whatsoever I know is just a few particles of sand in my hand. And, what I don't know is this infinite expanse of ocean." — Sir Isaac Newton

This is the story of Meera. She was born an ordinary child to ordinary parents in an ordinary place. Everything she saw was extraordinary. As soon as she became aware of herself, as a child, she was mesmerized by people whom she called mother and father. Love radiated from her mother in all directions, safety from her father. She wondered who they were, taking care of and loving her. She saw multitudes of people—in school, in markets—everywhere, people. Where did they come from and where were they going?

She looked up in the sky and was enchanted by its vastness. Where did the sky begin and where did it end, embracing her in its security like a cozy blanket. Wherever she looked, the sky seemed to expand in all directions. Whenever Meera felt sad, she stood under the open sky. Its immensity dwarfed her problems. She could no longer remain sad when the entire sky was showering love on her— such great love that her eyes would miss it if she was not paying attention. Some nights she would run from her house to a huge oak tree at the extreme end of the backyard and back to the main entrance of the house, enthralled, as well as puzzled, to find the moon, with all its brilliance, following her everywhere.

She would spend immeasurable time looking at all the bugs crawling on the ground, all the birds flying in the sky, all the fruits forming on the trees, all the leaves, flowers and plants sprouting from the soil and dirt, and all the humans walking on the earth as if those were the most wondrous beings she had ever imagined and seen. Long before it was taught in school, she knew that a caterpillar transforms into the most beautiful thing the eyes can ever see— a magnificent butterfly. A small seed can turn into the most majestic thing the mind can ever visualize—a tree. Just a single tree was an astounding universe for hundreds of different bugs, insects, and birds.

She saw herself surrounded by a mystery. From a seed, fruit was formed and that fruit was a mystery. From dirt, flowers rose, and those flowers were a mystery. From two people, came another being, and that other was a mystery. Every leaf, every tree, every person, every star, every planet, and every galaxy was a mystery.

The most fascinated thing she ever encountered was space and the movement of time. How did it come to be that she was surrounded by such enormous space and why didn't the stars fall from the sky... What kept them suspended in space... She tried to catch space in the palm of her hand but never could. How did time come into being... Yesterday, she was five, today five years and one day. She saw her limbs grow; her reason and understanding grew too. She was not doing anything to grow from a toddler to a child to a grown up. Everything was happening by itself, effortlessly, for her body and her mind. Everything was magical.

What was it—integrating her and the universe into one big harmonious unit... She herself was one whole, and she was also part of a bigger whole, humanity. All wholes, starting from the smallest unit, a cell, were part of, and eventually merged with bigger and bigger wholes, culminating into one grand whole, the universe. What was the integrating force in the cosmos which could not be seen or heard, it perplexed her. Its existence could be seen only with a sharp insight through various manifestations happening everywhere—stunningly beautiful and astonishingly intelligent—the flowers, the trees, the bugs, the insects, the birds, the animals, the humans, the stars, the galaxies, all bound together in one splendid universe.

Day by day, she became more and more obsessed with it. There was something tremendous about space which connected every-. thing: from a tiniest ant crawling on the earth to a distant star in deep space. Just the very thought would send her mind into the stillness of silence. She wondered at the phenomenon of nature. She could explain nothing. Nobody spoke about such things. When she saw people, trees, the sun, the moon, and the stars, she saw everything caressed by space, such a magnificent thing. She just didn't see people and things, but also the background on which everything was projected. She saw them, including herself, as animated images on a movie screen, except instead of a movie screen there was the screen of space. How the mind is so enchanted by moving images and imagines a story totally ignoring the screen on which images are projected, puzzled her.

As she grew older she could never see things as they appeared. She just didn't see the tree but also its internal structure—veins spreading from the roots to the top, providing nutrition to the entire tree—an organization of smaller wholes integrating themselves into bigger wholes, cells into roots and leaves, leaves into branches, and branches into the tree.

From early on she became aware of *'a thing in itself'* that was at the foundation of everything, hiding behind the veil of matter. Physical bodies were not just the physical bodies, but they were a manifestation of something grand. Whenever she saw another human being, she didn't see that person as a friend or a stranger but as a thing grand—a presence, carrying an elaborate, intelligent system of bones, organs, veins, and arteries which was at once elegant and precise, a system which was not manmade. She would look at people as if they were the most amazing marvels walking on the earth. She could never look at a face and not be overwhelmed by its grandeur, by the splendor behind a face, any face. Her head bowed in reverence and her heart filled with gratitude.

Her mother wondered about her whenever she found Meera looking at her strangely. When her friends asked her as to why she looked so alive all the time, she found it hard to explain. She learned early on that everyone did not see the world as she did. When they saw a tree, they just saw what was apparent, a tree. When they saw any other person, they saw a person, not a grand phenomenon carrying an elegant and subtle physical structure. Every morning she woke up in a warm embrace of the open and vast sky, and she would be enthralled every day, every moment of her life. When children her age were playing hide and seek, she played games of her own. She would pretend to be someone else watching from a distance, observing all her movements, thoughts, and desires—like she was watching a movie with Meera in it. It gave her immense thrill to see herself as such.

She failed to understand why everyone was worried about achieving something when they already were standing on the most glorious achievement—a presence and a body, and so naturally and effortlessly. She would spend countless hours looking at her hands, legs, and skin covering the body, so alive and throbbing. When she spoke, she was mesmerized by the sound that came out of her mouth. She would observe to see from where the sound was coming, a point hidden deep inside, not just the mouth. She knew that the mystery was inside. She would be moved with a powerful emotion. Something was inside the body, she was convinced, something grand and divine, so close, closer than the breath, yet the mind refused to acknowledge the holy presence lost in various pursuits.

She would stand still, not in dullness but in active silence and feel the presence, *'the thing in itself'*. The holy presence was not only inside her but was spread everywhere, harmonizing everything into one: from the limitless sky to the abundant earth, from the flowing rivers to the fathomless ocean, continuous and simultaneous. There was not a place where it was not. It was not the ordinary presence of a person but the presence of divine, the presence of life, of joy, of intelligence, and of love! The thought filled her with pride and gratitude that she existed as a part of it, glued with the rest of the world in some incomprehensible way. If she walked, creation walked with her. If she breathed, the entire cosmos breathed with her. Somehow this presence had divided itself in various ways and lived in self-forgetfulness.

Her mother knew she was different. There was a faraway look in Meera's eyes which seemed all too familiar to her. On a random day, she found Meera under a tree near the house, looking at the tree in such a way that it seemed she was looking at the soul of that tree and was in total communion with it. It was hard to distinguish if the tree was looking at her or she was looking at it. She had become the tree. There was not enough space for two. A look of bewilderment, love, compassion, and everything in between was in her eyes. A blissful completeness filled her face, a bliss which her mother thought impossible. For the first time in her life she wished if she could look at the world from her daughter's eyes. It was not the innocence of a child but the glory of knowledge. Spontaneous reverence arose in her heart, and she forgot that it was her child she was looking at. That day she knew she had lost Meera, for she belonged to the whole world.

PART THREE

I was not aware of the moment

when I first crossed the threshold of this life.

What was the power that made me open out into this vast mystery

like a bud in the forest at midnight!

When in the morning I looked upon the light

I felt in a moment that I was no stranger in this world,

that the inscrutable without name and form

had taken me in its arms

in the form of my own mother.

-Rabindranath Tagore

≈ 17 ≈

The Mystery of the Physical World

"Only when you drink from the river of silence, shall you indeed sing. And when you have reached the mountain top, then you shall begin to climb. And when the earth shall claim your limbs, then shall you truly dance." — *Khalil Gibran*

Radha woke up the next day to find rain clouds hanging in the sky. Sun showed its face for a while and then hid itself behind the shadows of the clouds. Radha was not herself. After dropping Abhi and Anya to school, she began to cook. That's what she did whenever she wanted to ponder. It gave her some time to think about what the monk and the woman had imparted to her in the past few weeks. She reflected on how her perception had changed within a span of few days. It seemed she survived an earthquake which destroyed her usual way of thinking. Now, she stood on an amazing knowledge which had no ground to begin with but held its place suspended on its own glory.

As the evening approached, she recognized a movement from the corner of her eyes. At first, she ignored it thinking it to be the shadows of the retreating day. But it persisted even into the night when everyone was asleep and the house fell silent. She focused on it. After a while it revealed a hole behind the movement in space. It grew bigger and bigger, and she felt herself being sucked into it. She closed her eyes, and after a moment she opened them and found herself surrounded by beautiful lush green fields of wheat. Few farmers were tilling the land at a distance. There was music in the air, and gentle soothing breeze was swaying her. She turned and met the gaze of the monk. It seemed he had lived there for ages comfortable, still, and calm.

Without wasting any time, she asked, "Everything I understand is related to the physical world. It has an overwhelming effect on me. If everything is conscious energy, then how does it get solidified? How do I come to exist as such and undergo intense forgetfulness about my real identity and start looking at the world as separate and external? Enlighten me on this."

"Let's try one more time," the monk began speaking. "It is a very complex subject. Everything ends in the physical world, but it starts in the transcendental world. What you see is nothing but an effect of the subtle higher dimension. There are only two things in the universe: matter and energy. *Matter* is what is seen as the physical universe, but reality is the *energy* hidden behind the apparition of matter. Each and every moment, energy is acting on matter. Do you believe there is nothing more than the physical world?

"I do feel what is seen is not all that there is."

"And how do you know that?"

"Because I have feeling and thoughts; they are not physical. There are times when I have such powerful thoughts that they annihilate physical needs for some time. When I am happy, I have tremendous energy. If I am sad, I do not want to eat for a whole day," she replied.

He nodded in agreement. "It is called *subtle world* of impressions and tendencies, of thoughts and desires. Just as your dream world is the manifestation of impressions taken from your waking life; similarly, physical world is also the manifestation of impressions taken from the subtle world. It is the field of energy and information. A field is as an abstraction expressing the forces of nature. It can take any form and shape in respect to time, space, and cause, such as gravitational field, electromagnetic field and so on. The invisible forces of thoughts, memories, and latencies—of mind, intellect, and ego—are expressed through the field of physical body.

"Your physical body is a chemical combination of few elements: ether, air, water, fire, and earth. But there is something profound working behind these elements, giving them their power and light. For example, eyes are the instruments of sight, but by themselves they are not completely independent as the organ of seeing. The organ of vision is the nerve center in the brain. Even if you have perfect eyes but your nerves are damaged, you will not see. So is the case with all sense organs: eyes, ears, mouth, tongue, and nose.

"The individuality principle in you, as Radha, is still working in the subtle body, giving it power. Though the power of your physical body is borrowed by the subtle body of your mind, intellect, and ego, they are bodies only, one gross and the other finer. Both are made of the same elements."

He tilted his head slightly to the left and looked at Radha with an expression that seemed to say he knew exactly what was going on in her mind. "Our gross body is easily perishable and any simple reason can disturb it. But the finer body of our ego is not so easily destroyed. Sometimes it degenerates, and at other times it becomes strong. Sometimes our mind is vigorous, sometimes weak. Every external thing affects us; we act and react to the world outside. When we speak to a person, we don't speak to the body but to the personality and character inside the body. Everyone is different because each has its own personal data recorded in the subtle field of ego and mind. It is the sum total of our personality. It carries inexhaustible energy, propelling us towards various activities, for fulfilling the desires we harbor in our hearts. These memories and thoughts are perceived as vibrations in the subtle realm of our mind. And later they are manifested as anger, depression, different aches and pains in the body, and also as our countless desires and fears, which eventually get manifested as our actions.

"The power of a focused mind is enormous; it is an intense field of electromagnetic energy that can attract anything towards itself and mold anything in any form, just like fire can mold iron. Iron can be compared to the physical body and fire to the force of thoughts. Nothing is more creative than a focused mind. It is the channel through which every little sensation is processed and manifested and acts as a store house of information in the form of thoughts and memories. Our mind is the center of a hurricane, a conceptual point drawing into itself the unknown forces."

He fell silent for a moment and looked intensely at Radha as if he was going to say something more profound. "But in reality everything is the same ocean, continuous and never ending. I am part of the same continuum, and you are part of the same continuum."

"Then, why do I feel my consciousness as different from yours, from the consciousness of this mountain and that sky?" Radha was doubtful of her own question.

The monk said, "Exactly that is how externality arises, due to a division between the consciousness of the seer and the existence of the seen, between the subjective consciousness and the objective reality. Though both are one and the same, they are seen and understood differently. There is a potent force in us—called *desire*, which in an intense urge to experience and create, crystallizes into a localized existence, which is then called *ego*. It is a desire that is born, not a child. You have to understand that your form and personality as an individual is only a stage in the process of evolution.

"I am a desire!"

"A desire is an inherent tendency of *consciousness* to move towards externalization, to seek what is the other. You are a shape taken by *a desire* at a spatial-temporal point and are created from the abyss of Infinite as a finite being. Just as sunlight can be centralized by allowing the rays of the sun pass through a lens. Similarly, *consciousness* arranges itself into a point and finitizes itself into individual egos and minds. We are intensely focused points of *consciousness*. We look different, act different and are born in different situations due to the fact that we have different desires. If we had same desires, there would be no different individuals but cumulative into one individual.

"I have said it before and I will say it again many times until you begin to grasp it. Ego is the first step in creation. Otherwise, nothing would manifest. It is the principle of egoism that forces various physical elements to integrate and organize themselves into a physical body, as you begin to think, act, and experience. It is the glue keeping your physical body together, so that you can safely exist as a person. For example, the castle you visited earlier, it's not independent of the wood, nails and so on. It wouldn't exist at all if the building materials are taken out of the structure."

"...and such a magnificent structure."

"In the same way, your body is a spatial shape taken by the ego principle in your consciousness. If you squeeze all the space in your body, you wouldn't have anything left to call the body. It is hollow and empty, but one which is filled with *ego*. If your body were not filled with *ego*, it would collapse in a moment, just like when you take the wood and nails from the building. It (ego) is not a substance. It is not tangible. It is a force centralizing into a point—not geometrical but conceptual, like the eye of a hurricane or the center of a tsunami. It is a point whose circumference is nowhere. The center is where your body is, but the essence of the person living in that body is omnipresent. We are intensely conscious of our bodily limitation by the power of affirmation that 'I am an individual; I love my individuality intensely and will preserve it at any cost.' This is *the original sin* as talked about religiously when Adam and Eve became aware of themselves as separate individuals. We have nothing in you except egoism. Every moment we assert it, consciously and subconsciously.

"It is quite complex and illuminating. I need to hear it many more times to process it," Radha remarked. Radha marveled at the fact that she always considered herself an intellectual and confined herself to the realm of intellect. It has its boundaries. It could take her as far as the reason goes and not beyond. She had limited herself till there. Now, in a flash, she became aware of something beyond where her reason could not go no matter how much it tried. It was only when she left it behind she became aware of the subtle dimension.

The monk smiled knowingly, "There is something beyond your intellect and ego, something much deeper and profounder than your subtle body, but that which exists within us. It is above the physical and beyond the subtle body you will find the absolute."

"But I exist as a physical body. How can I be more than my physical body?" Radha asked the monk, frustrated at her inability to grasp the truth.

"Think. If your physical body disintegrates—which it does eventually—your desire to create and experience does not die. Your thoughts and ideas are the forces in nature. A force can be transformed into another form, but it can never be destroyed; it is a scientific fact. So, are you gone when your physical form is gone?

"But my body has overwhelming power on me," Radha answered remembering how few months earlier she had cut her finger chopping vegetables. Such excruciating pain...so much blood! It brought tears in her eyes. After the pain had subsided, she felt foolish like a child screaming over nothing. She was terrorized by the physical pain and allowed it to take over her. In those moments of agonizing pain, she wanted to rather die than bear extreme sensitivity to raw, living tissue.

It brought the memory of yet another childhood incident as fresh as that day. She was five-years-old when she fell and hurt her knee while playing with her brother. There was blood, and she experienced pain for the first time. It shook her to the core. What was it...such unpleasant sensation. She realized something could happen to her body and she could experience very unpleasant sensation corresponding to it. It was not fun all the time. She felt betrayed by the whole universe and became sad. As a child, she became aware that she was connected to her body in some mysterious incomprehensible way. It followed her everywhere, somehow glued to her. She could not shake it off no matter how annoying it was. So she ignored it, but then realized she had to take care of it; otherwise, it could hurt her badly. The whole world became mysterious to her. She came into the world through a body, and then it started to control her. It was the most disempowering feeling she remembered.

The monk's compassionate voice brought her out of her reverie, "Let's start from what you see and recognize. You recognize a body with eyes, hands, legs, mouth, and so forth, like a machine with an organized system of cells and organs. Remember when you cut your finger. For the next few days you became aware of that little finger. How you took it for granted. It was always there but you never noticed. You needed the pain to see you had a finger."

Radha felt guilty. At the same time she marveled that he knew about the incident. Did he know everything about her?

"What a magnificent thing it is, the body, and how we abuse it. With pain we cannot ignore the body. Pain is a blessing to see that we exist; otherwise, we'd spend our life in numbness," the woman said.

She had come while Radha was deep in her childhood memory. Before Radha could open her mouth, the woman spoke again, "Are you just your hands, legs, liver and so on—an assembly of various physical limbs forming the body? If your body is just an assembly of parts, then can you, Radha, be created by putting together various parts of the body with some glue? What makes this body a person?"

Radha was too stunned to say anything.

"From where does the aliveness come in your body, the throb which is called life, the glory that only living brings—from where does it come?

Radha was too stunned to even think.

"Medical science can take an organ and transplant it in a different alive body. A dead body is just a corpse, and the value of a person cannot be discounted: his or her achievements, thoughts, inventions, dreams, the perfection, and the splendor. Great breakthroughs have been made in science, but even then nobody knows why the physical system works the way it does. We know how to fix it, but where is all this coming from. We come back to the same old question. What is the cause of a body? What we see is the effect."

Radha wondered at the enigma called the body. It is wholeness. It is love.

"Suppose, you have a strong muscular body; you cannot even lift your finger without the power of whatever it is in the background making it work."

Radha hung onto every word she uttered as if her life depended on it.

"Consciousness, Awareness, Life, Love—you can give any name. There is a presence in your body making you an integrated human being. Your identity is not this face or form. It is a point of awareness; a point which you have chosen to call Radha. No one can create the phenomenon of consciousness. It is the ultimate *thing in itself* without further differentiation. You can feel it indirectly through the phenomenon of thoughts, feelings, and desires. If physical, mechanical, or chemical combinations can produce consciousness then an object in motion, after some time, can generate a thought.

"Imagine the force in living organisms. It has the ability of infinite propagation, of evolving into new species, of covering the continents with vegetation. Desires and thoughts are also living organisms. There is immeasurable potential energy in them. Imagine the force in the words and ideas of poets, leaders, masters, and prophets. Their words continue to live and act even though they have been dead for years, even centuries. In fact their ideas have only grown and deepen with time, moving people to different heights. Observe how much of potential energy is there in the works of scientists like Albert Einstein and others which have revolutionized science to the present day and for future generations to come, or in some little verse of Shakespeare or Tagore. How can you say that once the physical body is gone, the person is gone? Thoughts and words are living cells, containing within themselves boundless energy, capable of making history, build nations, and destroy them.

"Still, you know nothing about how an idea is generated, how a thought is been thought, how living matter keeps on dividing and replicating itself. What is this intelligence at the background of your existence? In reality, you know nothing of the cause of the world, the indwelling reality."

"There has to be a way out to see though this maze?" Radha asked in anticipation.

The woman said, "Yes, if you can be present to your physical body, it can teach you about the universe and its workings because same principles work in both. It is a magnificent example of organic integration, precise and perfect."

"Organic integration,"

"If lots of pebbles are put together in order, they are mechanically connected. If you take one pebble out of the whole, it will change the arrangement but not affect the other pebbles as to their existence. But if there is a cut in your finger, you know it at once. If a part is taken out, the existence of the whole system's is adversely affected. This is vital and organic connection.

"There are trillions of cells in your body. You never feel yourself to be an infinite number of cells but always as a whole integrated person. Even if one cell is in distress, your entire body is in distress. Each cell is organically connected to every other cell notwithstanding the distance between them. The strength comes from the organic connection with the total system of the body. In the same way, everything is organically connected to the universe. The strength of an individual comes from his or her connection to the universal. You are an organism where every part is connected to every other part and is also complete in it-self."

Radha winced remembering the pain on cutting her finger. Even its memory brought such unpleasantness.

The woman continued, "Let's say, if your hand is amputated by some medical reason. You will still remain a whole individual. If your limbs were an essential part of your personality, then you would be thinking or feeling in lesser percentage. This proves clearly that you are independent of your physical body. You see only a part of the picture, not the whole thing. Your understanding works within this boundary of physicality. That is why appearances have assumed such great im-portance," she said simply, with a profound expression on her face.

Radha thought of Shalini, her friend from high school. In a freak ac-cident five years ago, her left hand was severed from her body. Doctors saved her, but they could not save her hand. After months of therapy Shalini learned to live with an artificial hand. But that didn't make her a lesser person. She was still the same gregarious, life-loving person she always was. Radha made a mental note to call Shalini. She hadn't talked to her in months, even though they lived in the same city.

A drizzle had become fully fledged outpouring of rain, and Radha stood still, oblivious of the wetness soaking her from the top to the bot-tom. She thought about the force in her body and at the same time felt protected by it.

It was the same night the monk reappeared before her. He had a heal-ing look on his face. There was sacredness about the whole moment. He was looking at her. What a look it was! Such compassion...so much love, like a mother has and even more than that. There was pain in those eyes. He was looking at her pain, and her pain was giving him so much more pain. Radha could see herself from his eyes. He made her glorious by his look. She felt ashamed of her own love. He didn't have to be there, but he loved her so much, he wanted to take the pain away. He bestowed peace on her. Tears rolled down her eyes. Such calm and bliss.

She looked at her body in reverence and wondered what doctors think when they open up a body to fix it. Do they think, it is just flesh and bones and not a person, or do they see the greatness of personality, the expansion of consciousness hiding behind the veil of solid matter? She again looked at her body as a child looks at it—in wonder—and began to see divine in every cell of her body. Her imperfections became divine. She realized her body was hers, yet not her. It was sacred.

"It is a gift from divine," the monk explained. "If you didn't have a body, what would you do, where would you go, how would you experience, and, most important, how would you think. You need an instrument to experience. You won't exist at all in the way you are existing now. It is holy. You are so loved, so looked after that you have been given a body to experience the truth. The biggest hurdle in reaching the truth—the mind-body complex—is absolutely necessary to experience it. The highest deception of Creation is the greatest manifestation of love. Your body reminds you of your existence in the physical world and introduces you to the higher intelligence working in the background. If you can be aware of your body and not lose it in mundane activities of self-interest, you will be able to see the divine through it. It is a tool to lead you back home."

They both stood there for a long time, locked in silence. He looked up at the sky. She also looked up at the sky. Its timeless beauty never failed to astound her.

For a moment Radha wondered where was she, lost within. Then she woke up. Oh, what a dream, she recollected to herself.

She looked at her body in amazement: her hands, her feet, the way they moved and expressed, or she expressed herself through the body, such magnificence. She wondered: 'Such great magic has been woven around me, but I refuse to see the beauty. The eyes to see, ears to hear, mouth to speak, and skin to touch; not only this, but also the intellect to understand and the heart to feel; this whole structure for me to experience, sacred and grand.'

She made a sound from her mouth, like a newborn experimenting with itself. She realized that the sound came from every fiber of her being; she was getting expressed through speech. A shift was taking place. Radha was becoming aware of the force that was making voice in the speech, hearing in the ear, and sight in the eyes. There was an undercurrent throughout her body which was always there.

She remembered two months earlier, she was having stomach surgery: The doctor gave me anesthesia, and I fell asleep. My body still went under the knife. It was cut and experienced invasion, but I did not feel a thing. I might as well be dead. My whole existence was negated. Where was I at that time? At exactly what day and time did I realize that it was not a body but me, and how did I get connected to it? There is a presence inside me, makes me alive, not just the mind but something which activates it, makes me the person I am, makes my intellect capable of understanding and my senses work. There is a mystery within myself I do not understand.

Radha looked outside. The night was wild and wet with rain. At the edge of her house stood a forest, cool even in the hottest months. Mysterious trees stood with age-old patience telling ancient secrets. She sat in her bedroom, picking at an apple, listening to the wind hurling itself into the night. The house was quieter than ever, with everyone asleep.

When she woke up the next day, she still had vivid memory of her conversation with the monk and the woman. She was feeling mildly intoxicated. Outside, a gentle breeze was playing with the trees. Night rain had made the air little chilly. Two birds were sitting on a beautiful magnolia tree, going from one branch to another, never still.

Radha picked up from where she had left off in the night: My ordinary mind with its finite powers cannot grasp the difference between the real and the unreal. The real has become unreal, like a dream, and something which I cannot comprehend has become real like a rock, even with its elusive nature. Who is this who comes to me and startles me, catches me when I least expect it? It smiles like a mischievous child, touches me and runs, urging me to find it. What or who is this?

Startlingly close and intimate like me, yet out of grasp, though always there, a feeling of silence...a feeling of presence...of eternity...of glory. It is the same feeling I get whenever I go to a place of worship, grand and divine. It looks at me with an unknown compassion, sharing its secret.

≈ 18 ≈

The Ancient View of the Human Body

"Thou hast made me endless, such is thy pleasure. This frail vessel thou emptiest again and again, and fillest it ever with fresh life. Ages pass, and still thou pourest, and still there is room to fill." —*Rabindranath Tagore*

Radha and Sam decided they would meet at a coffee shop after lunch. Sam was her friend from school and now a doctor. He was passionate about the alternative therapy more than the regular medicine. He deeply believed in the energy system, that ancient remedies had a potential to go mainstream. He was well versed in what ancient scriptures said about the body, mind, and its anatomy.

The restaurant was buzzing with people at that time of the day. They waited until the waiter brought their order of tea and samosas. Sam asked her, "Why do you want to know?

"It's for my new book," Radha replied.

Sam took a bite from his samosa and began speaking, "You asked for it. Medically we have a biological thing: the physical body made up of cells, arteries, muscle, organs and so on. Then we have a psychological faculty: our thoughts, feelings, emotions, and desires. We have the intelligence to understand, to decide, to reason, and to will. This function is attributed to the mind. Not everyone has the same intelligence. Different areas of the brain are seen activated explaining the different extent of intelligence in different people."

"How is a human being made from a cell?" Radha asked.

"Well, if we go to the beginning, it all began from the ability of the DNA molecule to replicate itself. Everything in nature is reproducing itself every moment. Even within our bodies every cell is replacing itself continuously, so that in seven to eleven years we have new bodies. None of the old cells are there. This ability to reproduce is of fundamental importance. Old leaves and flowers are shed in the fall to have new ones appear in the spring. Animals, insects, and humans reproduce continuously. Everything in nature has evolved over eons of time to have the current structure. Old ones die and new ones are born."

"What is the DNA?"

"It is the first living cell, which, for some mysterious reason, began to replicate it."

"Why?"

"This is one of the life's great mysteries. By fusing two cells an entire intelligent structure of a physical body comes into being, just like a giant tree comes out of a tiny seed. This can only be called a wonder." There was a look of deep reverence in his eyes.

"That's right. This is not just fusion of cells but something more astounding. No human thought has gone into it," she said excitedly.

"The organism of the *body* is integrated as such that all cells and organs in it work harmoniously as a complete unit. It is made up of trillions of cells; each one different from another but working in an organized way. Science has no idea how the cells in a body are able to organize themselves into a stomach, a brain, skin and so on, and start doing specified jobs at the same time, so that a human body can function as a person." There was a quaint expression on Sam's face which she could not read.

"So I have heard. May be they are intelligent living beings with mind of their own."

Before Sam could say something, Radha asked, "And what do the ancient scriptures say about the human being?"

"Are you sure you want to hear this," he seemed uncomfortable.

"Yes."

He began with academic anticipation, "Well, according to Vedanta, a physical body is the last step in the formation of a human being. We think we are a physical body because that's what we identify with. By the time this level comes, everything has become physical. It comes through five layers, but these layers are not physical." He took a sip from his cup of tea before proceeding further. "It is said that these layers are the urges of consciousness to move towards externality of experience," Sam whispered the holy secret. There was glorious look in his eyes.

"It is very intriguing. You have to explain further."

Sam looked outside the window on his side. It seemed it would rain that night. A couple, apparently much in love, was entering the restaurant.

"We have to start backwards from the physical body. It is sustained by the essence of food given to it. It has a beginning and an end, for as we know, people are born and die every day. We identify with our bodies so much that it's hard to believe that there can be another possibility, that we can exist without our physical bodies, that we are not just flesh and bones. We have what is called body consciousness. Throughout our lives we are driven by physical demands and work towards fulfilling them."

"This I understand," Radha said.

"To understand the next level, you have to first understand the third level. It is called mental sheath, the most sought after and worshipped—the glorious mind. Mind is considered superior to the body because if the mind does not work, the senses also do not give any kind of information. We would see things but not understand them. The principle connecting the mind to the body is prana. It is the energizing vital principal in our body. Do not confuse it with breath. It is more subtle than breath. Prana connects us to the physical world."

He stopped to catch his breath.

"We feel our body through the movement of energy in it. So many involuntary actions like circulation of blood, digestion of food, beating of the heart are going on, although we are not aware—all because of the movement of this vital energy. Our blood does not stop circulating, our heart does not stop beating, and our stomach does not stop digesting food. So many significant functions are going on without our intervention, effortlessly."

"What did you just say?"

"Effortlessly"

"I have heard this before. *Everything is taken care of, effortlessly,*" Radha muttered to herself.

"A person becomes a corpse when this energy is gone from the body. Our whole strength is the sum total of our prana. It is the fire within. We cannot make a corpse come to life by putting food in its mouth," he said triumphantly.

Radha looked at him with newfound admiration. He was indeed expert in his field.

"All new age teachers are giving so much emphasis on the energy of the body. They are talking about prana, and this is the second layer. Mind regulates the flow of prana in the body. Prana goes where the mind goes, and there is a corresponding effect on the body. If I am upset, I will not have any energy. If I am happy, my body will have tremendous energy. Such is the power the thoughts have on our bodies. Our minds are continuously communicating their impressions to our bodies through prana, urging us to become something or someone according to the desires we have. Positive thoughts have good effect and negative thoughts have adverse effect on us. That is why so much emphasis is given on thought power, because ultimately our thoughts, especially strong ones, become our actions."

Both of them were distracted by some noise. They looked outside the restaurant. Two teenage boys were fighting with each other. Sam continued after watching them for few minutes.

"The fourth layer is ego. Actually, the body, prana, and mind come into existence through ego. It is the cohesive force bringing the body and mind together, as well as keeping it intact. According to ancient wisdom, a physical body is the gross manifestation of subtle tendencies and desires, which are basically thoughts that have come into being through the individuality principle in us. What is ego and how it comes into being still remains a mystery."

Sam began to fiddle with his napkin. He seemed distracted.

Radha was amazed. She had heard the same things from the monk and the woman.

"What about the fifth layer, or the first?"

"I wish I knew. It is said that the first one is the *Soul, Spirit, Higher Self, Universal Consciousness,* which, in an urge to experience the world of space and time, has condensed itself into *cosmic ego,* then *individual ego, intellect, mind, and body.* It is the deepest most, inner most, bottom most principle in the formation of a human being, and also in the formation of the universe."

"The seat of consciousness," Radha said under her breath.

Sam's eyes widened. He knew something else was going on. "Normally, human understanding is limited to the ego-body. In fact, only highly aware people are conscious of ego and its play. Ordinary person is limited to the material aspect of existence and doesn't even look beyond that, doesn't even wish to look further. His understanding of the world is limited to its appearance, and he considers himself a physical being." Again, he looked at her intensely trying to get a glimpse of the mystery.

"Ah, the Seduction of the Mind...Do you think yourself as a physical being or more than that?" Radha asked.

"I'd like to think that I am more than that. All scriptures point that. All enlightened souls give the same message. But there is an overwhelming effect of matter, space, and time on my mind and body. Wherever I see, I see space, people, and earth. I see time passing. I feel pain when my body gets hurt. I feel hunger for food, thirst for water. I look for recognition from my peers and a socially well-placed life. These demands are so overpowering that even if I want to believe in more than the body concept, my mind brings me back. My family, my friends, my work is my world. As far as I am concerned, this is my existence. The rest are intellectual talk. There are moments when I feel the truth beyond matter, but those are rare moments. No matter how much I try to recapture them, once they are gone means they are gone."

"What moments?"

"Moments of highest ecstasy, a look from a loved one, the immediate moment at the peak of success, and also moments of utmost despair when everything seems to stop, time becomes timeless. In the presence of imminent danger when fear throws you off guard and you become aware of a timeless dimension in the stillness of the present moment, for split of a moment, like in a crash."

"Were you in a car crash?"

"Yes, several years ago. I lost a friend too." His eyes looked distant.

"Radha, what made you ask these questions. Is it just your book or something else?" He glanced at her inquisitively.

Radha smiled guiltily but collected herself quickly.

"Curiosity has its own reasons for existing."

They sat there for another half hour taking about their families and work before saying goodbye.

≈ **19** ≈

The Phenomenon

"What in the body's tomb doth buried lie; Is boundless; it is the spirit of the sky, Lord of the future, guardian of the past." —Carl Rice

Radha was totally exhausted by the time she reached home. She wanted to take a nap before Suraj came back. It was his turn to pick up the twins from their nanny. As she stepped in her room, she caught her reflection in the mirror above the dresser.

She looked at her body, the biological thing—a physical field. She took a deep breath. As she became aware of her breath, she also became aware of the connection between her body and mind. Breath was the thread. She took another deep breath, and then another. Slowly, she became more and more aware of the silence around her. *Breathe in, breathe out.* Silence surrounded her, cradled her with an overwhelming force, so strong and fragile. In the stillness of her mind, amazing knowledge came. She became illumined. She realized with crystal clarity that everything was born out of Silence. With conscious breathing her mind became still, like magic. *Breathe in, breathe out.* It was only when her mind became calm, creative action began. This calmness was not the stillness of inertia but the fathomless silence of within.

She thought: I have a treasure in my hand and I refuse to use it. I am not even aware about its existence. Silence around me turns alive as I breathe. It breathes with me. It caresses me, loves me like nobody else has ever done, not even myself. It is filled with the awareness of its being. I am not alone... never was. It has always been with me, through the ages... and will always be. All glory of life belongs to it. It is Silence's will that works in all. The endless Silence is eternally eloquent and thousand words cannot articulate it. There is nothing to be done, nothing to be said, just be aware of it, which is so deep that it is resounding everywhere, every moment. It has amazing beauty and timelessness. It is Existence. It is Eternity. It is God.

Words fail me. Words cannot convey silence; they only diminish it. It is the beauty in beautiful, the power in powerful, the intellect in intelligence, the glory in glorious. Tears fill my eyes. I cannot contain such pleasure. It overwhelms me. I have to think, so that Silence goes away. I have been searching for greatness, for completeness, for perfection all my life, and, now, I have come to a point from where it all starts, with each step it gets clearer. My seeking has given me some answers, some ground to stand upon, to continue the journey. I feel strong, powerful, and elevated. I sing and dance. I do not know what else to do. Joy is overtaking me and I am forgetting myself. My little body is not equipped to contain such pleasure; it can break and explode anytime.

As she was contemplating and reflecting on Silence, Radha found herself in a familiar room with no furniture. She saw a door and tried to open it. It seemed stuck. On second try, it opened and she found herself on the snow clad mountain. Everything was pure and white with snow, but she did not feel any cold. At a distance she saw the woman, sitting deep in meditation. She opened her eyes and looked straight at Radha. Instantly Radha felt overwhelmed with a feeling which could only be called bliss—because it was more than happiness, more than joy, and more than love.

Radha asked, "Why don't I see the structure of my body as perfection. It is so intriguing. There is a physical structure, there is a psychological structure, and there is a spiritual structure. There is a body, there is a mind, there is an intellect, and yet there is beyond."

The woman said, "You, as a body, are filled with space. And space cannot be empty because you, as a *being*, are the one within the space! That you are capable of thinking, feeling, and reasoning is evidence enough that *being* is capable of thinking, feeling, and reasoning as well.

When *being* stirs with notions, *it* becomes the mind. *Being* vigorously asserts itself through your soul and the soul of each person.

"*You* experience through the body-mind complex. These are the instruments. *You* are the innermost principle. *You* endow the body with life and forget that it is not identical with you. At the deepest level of creation there are no bodies, no boundaries. Underneath, everybody is same. Your personality is not a physical matter but a continuous movement of the mind. The same force is the essence of all minds. We all are powered by the universal."

Suddenly, Radha had a remembrance as if she was just waking up from some kind of amnesia. She knew about it but had forgotten, and now which can only be called intellectual illumination, she remembered and understood.

"Just as when I pour coffee in different cups, it becomes my cup and your cup, but in essence it is coffee only," Radha remarked.

The woman had a joyous expression on her face. Her hair flowed in gentle breeze like a waterfall, her face shone in its own brilliance. "You are a presence animating this body. You are the centre of consciousness. *And* your center is everyone's centre. It is from here the awareness of the world arises. You are pure *being*, the substratum of all names and forms!"

Radha remained quite still as the impact of the words hit her. She became aware of the stillness surrounding the majestic mountain peaks covered with snow. The view was breathtaking. The stillness held her in its womb. Then she entered it—the stillness of silence and the expansion of space. She was no longer Radha but had expanded into space. She saw and realized with crystal clarity that space was a throbbing being. It was scintillating with awareness, filled with unadulterated joy. One more time, she was thrown in the space of Eternity where she remembered nothing and forgot nothing. Thoughts vanished and she was left in a suspended state where nothing remained, except herself, and love. She felt she was going to explode any minute.

"How do I come to the terms with these astounding principles? They threaten to smash all my beliefs. I am resisting the new way of thinking." Radha mustered enough courage to say.

"You don't have to worry. Everything is effortless. Right now you are working through your intellect, which is within the realm of your individuality *and* Truth threatens to dissolve your individuality. Always remember, the power of pure knowledge is far more powerful than the power of intellect and ego. Universal is more powerful than the individual."

"This is frightening. I am scared." Tears were rolling down her cheeks.

"See it this way, there is something beyond your intellect, for there is a higher knowledge than human understanding. It will come to you when you are ready. You don't need an effort to wake up from sleep."

Radha tried to think of a way to get to consciousness higher than the mind but was lost in a labyrinth of thick fog, of concepts and ideas.

"How can you be so sure?" Radha asked like a lost child. She saw the monk magically appear beside the woman. His sudden appearances at random moments had ceased to startle her. They both looked as if they had known each other for ages.

The monk answered, "Otherwise how does knowledge arise in us. Knowledge is not the function of intellect. Intellect is only an outcome of the individual psychological principle, Ego. It always assumes that an individual exists. It is not cosmic; if it is, then we create knowledge, not unveil it. It is a great mystery beyond human comprehension."

"How can I access *it*?" Radha was still dazed and intoxicated. A new way of understanding was taking place.

The monk nodded indicating he was aware of her restlessness and said, "The bad news is we cannot access it by going anywhere or doing anything, because it is not located at some particular place or time. We cannot even understand it, for it is the preconception of even the act of understanding. It is too immense for human mind. It is like telling icebergs and glaciers about the ocean when they themselves are the ocean. *But* the good news is we can experience it by *being it*. Right here and now at the exact place we are, we can be it, for it is located everywhere at all times. We can raise our individual ego to cosmic mind through contemplation, reflection, and meditation. When we become aware of our presence, self-knowledge comes on its own. When questions arise in our mind, answers are not far behind. What we seek, we shall find. This is the law."

Instantly, a veil fell off as understanding pierced Radha, and she experienced an insight unparalleled in the world.

"Above the Ego is the Absolute! The Alpha and the Omega! The most talked about, The Holy Grail!" She exclaimed joyously as she watched the monk go deeper and deeper into the space before disappearing all together. The woman followed him.

That was the last thing Radha heard from them that day. She thought about *consciousness* hiding behind her intellect, urging her to think and imagine all kinds of things. What she was experiencing could be the trick of her mind. Still, she could not imagine what she had not experienced. A hallucination could not be so alive and profound. It could not beckon her with such an overpowering intensity. If it was a trick of her mind, it was a good trick. Universe was whispering the ancient secrets in her ears.

That day as Radha slept, she had the strangest feeling that she was very close to the truth, so close that she could touch it with the naked body of her soul; she could feel it in the scent of her breath. The woman was waiting for her on the snow clad mountain as Radha closed her eyes.

"This is the divine truth. You have to contemplate it many more times before you can have a tiny grasp of it. Just like every cell in your body is part of and connected to your entire body; similarly, every single person is part of and connected to the entire cosmos, forming a bigger organism. Everything, including me and you, are fluid touching each other at the essential level. Where one ends and another begins cannot be known. The entire universe is one big continuum, a homogenous existence. If something happens in one part of the universe, the entire universe is aware of it. There is no such thing as a private act. Whatever actions we perform and whatever thoughts we entertain, the universe is aware of it and is also affected by it. If one person is happy, the entire cosmos becomes happy. If one person becomes sad, the whole universe feels the sadness. Even if a small needle pierces the tip of a finger, the entire body feels the pain."

Radha gasped, at the same time, felt love. Not of something or someone; it was simply love—naked, intense, and pure, without any root or cause.

After a moment or an eternity, the woman said, "The vast atmosphere around us is the environment which upholds us, sustains us. We are inseparable from it—the air we breathe, the water we drink, and the sunlight we bask yourself in. It does not matter if I am a man or a woman, or what my cultural and religious beliefs are, ultimately, I am coming from this planet."

"Countries are only conceptual boundaries for administrative convenience. I knew that," added Radha.

"Observe what an overwhelming effect our country, our education, our religion and beliefs have on us, so much that we cling to them as our realities and refuse to see such a simple fact that we are coming from the cosmos. This is the highest seduction of the mind. And we love every part of it. From the time we are born we are always something in terms of something else. We are never our true self—unmasked and clear. We are a child or a parent, a genius or ignorant, a Hindu, a Christian, a Moslem, or a Jew and so on. List can go on endlessly. These are our false personalities, but they—social, psychological, and cultural realities—make our lives. They overwhelm us; keep us in a state of subconscious tension, so that we never see that we belong to the whole humanity. This is the biggest deception, the highest betrayal, *and* also the perfect love. A diamond is covered in layers and layers of sand and dirt, keeping the precious stone hidden."

"I am charmed by my prejudiced individuality," Radha added.

"If we look at Earth from outer space, we do not see different countries, families, or cultures but one whole planet. Widening our view, we see the entire solar system, not just Earth. Stretching the imagination further and further, we come to a staggering realization that there is no I or you, my family or your family, my desires or your desires, but one universe—vast and cozy, the one filled with joy."

Radha felt dwarfed by the enormous truth the woman spoke and felt herself spread endlessly in all directions. She had always considered herself a daughter, a friend, a spouse, a writer, and a mother. Her relationships and her education defined her whole life. They confined her. She was always role playing depending on the person she was with. When she was with herself, she reflected on those various relationships and roles.

"We all belong to one and the same family, the one which extends beyond the planets, the stars, and the galaxies. It encompasses the entire cosmos. We are the force in the universe, concentrating ourselves into visible forms of existence..."

"...of human beings, trees, mountains, rivers, planets, galaxies and the very cosmos itself," Radha finished, bringing the pearls of wisdom from the abyss of remembrance as a chill went down her spine.

When silence subsides, intellect comes, and with intellect comes reasoning, noise, and activity, and then disconnection with reality. There were times when Silence overtook Radha and she went beyond her intellect, but it did not last for long. Then it was back to disconnection, doubt, and fear. She questioned her mind as to what was real and what was unreal. In her dreams she felt Life was looking at her; it penetrated her soul and made her aware that there was a mystery, and she was in the middle of it. All she had to do was enjoy it. To solve it, she had to apply the mind. Then it would become an effort. She was not just part of it but she herself was the mystery to be revered and celebrated. She was the reason mystery existed in the first place.

Her heart began pounding when, still at a distance, she saw the monk coming towards her from behind a tree. She bolstered up enough courage to walk halfway towards him. He continued the conversation as if there was no break.

"I will say it again: the ultimate secret[3]. Just like there is an individual mind and ego behind your physical body, there is cosmic mind and ego behind the physical universe—as in microcosm, so in macrocosm. Just as your body is a spatial shape taken by the physical elements, glued together by the power of your ego principle, so is the universe a spatial shape taken by the physical elements, glued together by the power of cosmic ego. The phenomenon integrating your physical body is the same that integrates the universe. Just as your physical body is an

---

[3] Inspired by Madhu vidya in ancient Hindu text Upanishads.

organic integration where each and every cell is harmoniously working towards the overall existence and maintenance of your body, so are *you* also a cell in the body of the universe, organizing with others, into different integrating centers, moving towards the harmonious working of the universe as whole. All planets are revolving around the sun in the Milky Way galaxy, and the galaxy together with other galaxies is moving in some direction, propelled by the central force of the entire cosmos. Every point in space and time is this center, so that when you touch anything, you are touching the center of the universe."

Radha went numb with awe, her mind registering only bewilderment.

The monk continued in his most secretive voice, "There is an ultimate phenomenon present in creation. It is called Consciousness, it is called Joy, and it is called Existence. It is the only truth there is. The principle of consciousness is animating all creation: from the awe-inspiring physical universe to all individuals and to every little creature. The same phenomenon is animating the objective and the subjective aspect of the world. The objective is organically related to the subjective. A part is not constitutionally separate from the whole, and the whole is not in any way different from the part. It is the reason any understanding, any thought, any desire arises in you. It is the reason any action is performed by you. On physical level, it operates as gravitation and electromagnetism; on psychological level, as love; on cognition and thinking level, as integration of thought. Ultimately, it operates as the connecting link between the subject and the object. When the sun rises, it also rises within you. When the wind blows, it also blows inside you. If some event, good or bad, happens in any part of the world, it also happens inside you—for you are the cosmos. *You are the phenomenon* present in the universe! You are completeness. You are wholeness. You are love."

A tremendous silence descended on Radha as she contemplated on the greatest secret she was told, her body becoming lighter and lighter till she could hardly feel it.

She thought: I am a spark of eternal life. When I take a breath, the entire universe with its stunning beauty is breathing. The being who is nearer to me than myself is not some stranger with supernormal powers but my own higher self. It resides in the heart of all beings! Sometimes the higher self is so near that I can touch it, and sometimes so far away that reaching it becomes impossible. The distance of ages of conditioning separates us, but love brings us closer in a moment. My heart is overflowing with gratitude. What is the magic, this higher self weaves around that, in a flash, everything becomes clear, and then it is gone, with only a blissful memory which tugs at my heart for more and more.

Radha woke up experiencing enhanced tranquility. She was engrossed in thinking beyond her own mind. She was experiencing things which made it difficult to ignore the existence of another dimension. So many times, in the night, the transcendental dimension had come, but she had either ignored it or distorted it due to her lack of understanding. With time she has learned to acknowledge it without the feeling of fear. Now, she was beginning to embrace it, and what an embrace! So much love, such power comes from within. Never in her wildest dream did she think that such feeling could exist: feeling of completeness, of being embraced by the cosmos as if she is the only person in the universe and the universe loves her totally. Existence looks at her as a mother looks at her child. She cannot handle so much joy. Words diminish the expression.

That day she did her meditation, cleaned the house, shopped for groceries. She even called Shalini. She saw a cart vendor selling vegetables. Fresh tomatoes, chilies, ginger, cucumber adorned his cart. She was looking at him from the patio window at a distance. There was tiredness on his face worn out by years of labor. He may not have known comfort which material things bring, but he held himself very straight. There was an odd dignity about him that only indifference brings. Perhaps he had old parents and family to look after, tucked away at home. Radha looked at him in amazement: his face, his eyes, the way he was walking. His hands were moving with dexterity when he weighed the vegetables. There was life in those limbs and face. When she looked in the eyes, she became aware of a personality working in the shadows, propelling him to do activities of the world, to dream, to hope, to laugh, and to cry. She tried to look behind the face, those eyes, behind his individual ego. There was Universal hidden somewhere behind him. Did the vendor know what he were... a force, a marvel, and a wonder? From a distance he was a human. Under a microscope he was cells, molecules, atoms, and particles. At a farther range he was part of the community, the country, and the universe. He had so many layers, like an onion. An objective view revealed an organized system of layers that was alive at every level—astonishingly intelligent, elegantly precise, and stunningly beautiful. Radha realized that the human identity was only a layer but a vital one, in a much deeper and wider reality.

It was an unusually bright sunny day with the touch of spring in the air. There was great delight among the trees and the birds. But vegetable cart vendor went by without noticing the delight in the air too wrapped up in his joy and sorrow, which belonged to him and him alone. His stories owned him, possessed him in a way that he totally lost sight of the immense and the beautiful, in plain sight, waiting to be touched, and to be made love to.

Meera
Written By: Radha

≈ *2* ≈

Gravity

"Truth is the offspring of silence and unbroken meditation." —Isaac Newton

As Meera grew older and found out about the laws of physics, she did not lose the sense of wonder, as so many grownups do. She learned that the earth obediently revolves around the sun following the law of gravity. It was a force that kept the planetary bodies in their respective places. But she wondered how such law came into being. She tried to imagine what would happen if the law of gravity stopped working, then realized that everything would collapse. The entire universe would fall into an infinite abyss. But where—that she failed to understand. She obsessed about it day and night.

Her joy knew no bound when she learned about Issac Newton, Albert Einstein, Werner Heisenberg, and other physicists who had tried to solve the riddle of the universe. She felt reverence and gratitude for these scientists, and then these feelings of appreciation and awe were followed by immense love for them. Despite the fact that they were no longer in their bodies, she felt their friendly presence all around her. She could hardly contain herself thinking about the discoveries they made, and how much love and desire for truth they must have had to come to such staggering discoveries. She wished she'd been born a hundred years earlier and been able to interact with such brilliant minds.

Many times over the past few years, she'd felt she breathed the same air as they had. At those times, the boundary of space and time no longer existed. She was convinced that everyone who had ever lived from the beginning of creation was still living in the same space, just in a different dimension; the boundary of space time was ethereal, and she could break it and experience the elusive dimension in a flash. Nevertheless, a mystery remained, one she had to solve, one which involved no one but herself.

When she grew up, she became a physicist. She still wondered at the phenomenon of nature. Her rational mind wanted to know the cause of everything. Yet another part of her mind wondered why there needed to be cause for anything in the universe. Couldn't a thing exist by itself, but her rational mind did not permit such thinking, at least not for long. That part of her brain thought in terms of time, space, and causation. That was how she was conditioned to think.

She was sure what she saw as the immense, astronomical universe was a superimposed reality. The existence of cosmos itself suggested the presence of a higher intelligence. In her dreams, she would often find herself floating in space. There—she was not an insignificant being but would expand to become the entire universe. It was her home. She would walk through the universe as if she were walking in her home. Space was vast and immense, so was she. She and the universe were blended together in one whole. She visited black holes, gateways, parallel universes, as though they were different rooms in her house. Those were not just dreams, fancies of her imagination, but she felt their solidity. If she was imagining, the fact of imagination was evidence enough of its truth, because, she told herself, mind cannot imagine what was not possible. Everything in existence first had its birth in the mind, had existed in countless minds as a potentiality for ages to make it possible. That was how anything was created—*from a thought.*

She recalled an essay she'd written for admission into a prestigious science research institute in California: We live in two worlds simultaneously. First is the world of science, through which we observe things as they are, objectively. A human body is a human body. Whether it belongs to the president of the country or a mentally challenged person—it does not matter. It has the same internal structure and network of bones, veins, arteries, skin, and organs. If a physician cuts a single human body, it gives information about all bodies. Science does not differentiate; it does not judge or pass opinions. That's the reason it has been able to make such astounding discoveries and cures.

Then, there is the world of human perception tainted by personal prejudices, likes and dislikes, mine and yours. Generally we identify with this group. When we see a human, we see him or her as a friend or a stranger, not as any other being similar to me. We never look objectively. There is no other way to look at people and things except through the lens of me and mine, at least not in the present world of society where we live side by side with global terrorism. It shows we are far away from the truth. This perception extends into other things—my family, my community, my country, my religion. We identify with these and fall into the everyday struggle of mine and yours, and let the beauty of existence pass by unnoticed, unrevered. And we miss the joy of feeling embraced by the universe, sheer delight of watching a flower bloom in full glory—simple pleasures of life, from moment to moment.

Until the time we are not able to raise our awareness to the world of science, we would be condemned to live in the world of joy and sorrow, of heaven and hell, not as punishment from some higher hand but by our own folly, like children fighting over silly toys. We are so captivated by the toys that it has become impossible to turn away from such an enchanting and intoxicating dance. Turn we must, though, if we are to live harmonious and enriching lives. The existence of the world is not the problem. The problem is our idea about it. We have to learn to observe every phenomenon working within us without any physiological function operating in the background. Then only we can hope to have some spark of true knowledge.

Her essay brought her acceptance at the research institute. Ten years later she was still there. She knew the problem she wanted to solve but could not find a way out of the mystery that surrounded it. From whatever angle she looked, whatever observations she made, whatever experiments she performed, she did it from behind the wall of Meera. She knew that difficulty stemmed from her intellect only; it prevented her from looking at the truth face to face. She took pride in her heritage of being a scientist and found herself confronting the biggest limitation of science. Scientific inquiry had reached into the atoms, electrons, and even energy, but it ignored one essential piece of the puzzle—the scientist. It denied the existence of the one who was experimenting and observing. It was not possible to observe an objective reality without an observer. She realized there was a certain awareness within her that had the capacity to observe—*she herself.* In every observation she made, she always remained unobserved. Human consciousness was not understood by science, so it was ignored. She tried to console herself that the frustration she felt was similar to all the outstanding minds who had also tried to solve the riddle. She felt responsible that science was not complete. It ignored the subjective side of the world, so captivated it was in trying to solve the riddle of the objective world, even though it knew that the objective and subjective were different sides of the same coin. For a long time she'd realized the necessity for science to grow a new dimension that went inwards, the side which was normally claimed by religion. At the same time, she was proud, that science did not pretend to know everything. It accepts the boundary of the known, and that something would always remain unknowable. Here her intellect failed her.

In the following months, she became aware of another world, a transcendental world, one which was always there in the background, containing within itself all dimensions of space and time. On a random day, her perception shifted and became clearer, and she began to understand. Layers of the mind began to peel off, and she was left totally open, proud, and glorious. Peace began to permeate her.

It was during one of those moments of heightened perception that she realized the beauty of numbers and arithmetic. Though language could be expressed differently, letters could be arranged to make good words and bad words, a word could carry different meaning for different people, Mathematics, on the other hand, was precise. Six plus six would always be twelve, every time. If six plus six was twelve, so were five plus seven and various other permutations and combinations. She could not decorate numbers with her ideas and concepts. They did not show preference to her. Language was human; mathematics was divine. She reflected how the human world was like a language, which could be adorned with ideas and opinions. Reality was like mathematics, precise and universal, always there, always embracing. Meera loved this dimension of mathematics, its aloofness from the hindrances of the words and language, existing without the limitations of ideas; a dimension which was immeasurable and immense, one that always filled her with joy.

What she realized about gravitational force threw her into the heights of wonder. As a student of science, she knew its history and how Sir Isaac Newton discovered it and what it meant in scientific terms. Stars and planets were not suspended in space but were strategically arranged with relative pull upon each another, keeping themselves in their respective places. This knowledge always mesmerized her. The wonder was not the gravitational force, but the mystery which could set such astronomical bodies in a precise and harmonious relationship. The perfection in the cosmos was simply too immense for human mind. The gravitational force was still a wonder, because, ultimately, no one knew what the mysterious pull was.

She observed the organic interconnection of all things in the universe; it kept her in awe throughout her life, and how it was so evident in gravitational force. It clearly proved that things (matter) were not scattered in space independently. She was in her room and there was a tree outside; they did not exist independently. If there was gravitational force, then there was interconnection in the universe. Some medium has to be there to make it all work. Imagine the pull exerted by the full moon on the ocean. Waves of high tides reach up to embrace the moon. Look at the sun. It is some light years away from the earth and look at the gravitational attraction. It intensely compels planets to move around in their orbits.

The deeper she went into the world of matter, the more insight she gained about the stupendous secret: the secret of organic interconnection among all bodies. She saw organization every step of the way: whether it was the formation of a rock, the structure of a star, or the working of a physical body. Uniform. Continuous. Simultaneous. She realized that there still existed deep space whose presence was not known even with the most powerful of telescopes, not yet, but its presence exerted a vital, living influence on everyone.

She reflected that it was not a secret that family, friends, and even strangers affect each other in various intensities. Everyone acts and reacts to each other. Action on one part and reaction on another part makes it imperative that there is a connecting link going on between minds too. The space between people and things cannot be empty. It has to be filled with higher intelligence and love. When it works in people, they feel love and affection, and repulsion too. Why is there a need to know another person, to exist on a social level... Why is one engulfed with goodness when one meets a friend... No one is glued to another with some substance. Yet everyone, in relationship with each other, forms a bigger body—from an individual to families to communities. This integration has nothing to do with physical distance; it is a totally different phenomenon. Meera contemplated that science and religion, both are looking at the same thing but perceive it differently. Gravity is the function of love and joy.

More Meera reflected on scientific discoveries throughout the centuries, more she found herself falling into the fathomless abyss of wonder, which, at the same time, kept on throwing her to the astonishing heights of increased wonder. Depths were calling on heights and heights were calling on depths.

Meera thought: Whatever we found—molecules, atoms, electrical charges—there was always something, a thing in itself, whose nature could not be comprehended, which could not be seen or touched, an enigma which had always baffled scientists (and is still going on). Nothing is solid, including me. Everything I see and everything I touch is basically vibrations vibrating at different speeds. But why are they vibrating in such a manner, and how do they affect me? Are they my friend or enemy?

Meera was getting more and more restless every day. She was still startled, as she was the first time, to realize that she was surrounded by electromagnetic fields. It still infused her with ceaseless wonder each and every time she thought about it. She could see the objects, but the fields surrounding them were not visible to the naked eye. The fields could not be defined, but their power and beauty could only be felt. What more evidence was needed, she questioned herself, to see the existence of higher intelligence penetrating each and every point in space and all beings.

And still I go on pursuing some activity, ignoring its presence, in search for something wonderful. It is in plain sight, but I choose not to look. It is only when I begin to acknowledge It, It embraces me. My mind goes numb with wonder, language fails to express. 'What a wonder' is all I can say as I realize the essence of energy and vibrations. *It is joy.* The fact that energy is vibrating is evidence enough that it is alive. My essence is the same as of the energy. It is neither a friend nor an enemy, because it happens to be *me*. It affects me to the extent I affect myself!' My mind is hushed to see such integration, such wholeness. I surrender in silence as I realize that the higher intelligence exists, inexorable, unabated, unmitigated, omnipresent, the same characteristics that God is supposed to be endowed with.

On a summer night of June in the year 2008, when Meera slept, little did she know that her life was going to be changed forever. That was the night she felt terror, and she screamed.

She was deep asleep and woke up after an hour, rested and re-freshed. As soon as she woke up, she felt herself suspended on noth-ing. The whole creation was there with her in that room. In fact, at the exact point where she was! All the people who had ever existed were there. She was terrified and felt that she was confronted with death. Terror was not even the word to describe what she felt. It was terror so real that all experiences put together were unreal in front of it. She screamed and ran out of the room, down the winding staircase. There she stopped for a minute, feeling the panic pierce through her. The suspension continued for some time before dissolv-ing in silence. She knew something extraordinary had happened. Existence was there with her! It disappeared after a minute, but that one minute was more profound than her whole life. She saw a wholly new dimension. She came back to her room. Everything was as it was. And everything had changed. The reality of her present life turned into a dream, and she suspended on nothing became real where only she existed.

It began to happen frequently in nights when she would be deep asleep and then wake up refreshed. One night, she woke up in the middle of the night to find the 'feeling' overlooking her the whole time she was asleep. In a flash, it entered her head. It could only be expressed as a 'feeling' due to limitation of words. She experienced, in a split second, the feeling was coming from inside her. It was not something external but resided within! As soon as it entered her, she was engulfed by overwhelming love for the whole humanity. She felt bliss, followed by intellectual illumination. So much knowledge came on its own as if waiting, like a beloved waiting to made love to. It was not an experience. It was a revelation.

As she became more and more familiar with the feeling, she be-gan to acknowledge and finally embrace it. Her whole being began to vibrate with a new energy. She would keep a question in her mind and wait for it to be answered. Answers would come unexpec-tedly, anywhere, at odd times, through mysterious channels, without any apparent cause—sometimes in form of epiphanies, sometimes intellectual illuminations, and sometimes in flashes as remembrances which were somehow forgotten.

She realized there was a dimension to the world which everyone ignored. Everyone believed that the world was real, that their mundane pursuits were real. Their triumphs and tragedies were real. But the universe, as it was, without any pursuit was so beautiful, so perfect. It had so much to offer. There was so much happiness, so much love, and so much energy in it.

Another night, she woke up to find everything inside her vibrating at an infinite speed, and she was totally still. Her entire body had become energy vibrating at infinite speed. What a wonder! She realized that she had created the rip in space-time.

Later she wrote in her journal: I feel the coziness of space around, like a blanket protecting and loving me. Earlier I was so mesmerized by the objects that I failed to see the space around. Now when I look, I see space everywhere, even inside the objects, not the space that is measured—it is endless space. I see it in a flash, a swiftness which my eyes cannot follow. It leaves me empty of thoughts and fills me with joy. I am left wondering how such a thing could be. I profoundly feel that I am not alone, never was. The whole creation is with me. It is the same intelligence which makes me alive, makes me exist in the first place. Whatever is me, breathing and living in me as me, is the same as this living and breathing phenomenon outside. It is not possible to articulate in words. The only tribute I can give is silence.

.

PART FOUR

In whose speech is my voice,

in whose movement is my being,

in whose skill is in my lines,

whose melody is in my songs, in joy and sorrow.

I thought he was my very self, coming to an end with my death.

Why then in a flood of joy do I feel him;

in the sight and touch of my beloved?

This 'I' beyond self I found on the shores of the shining sea.

Therefore I know,

this 'I' is not imprisoned within my bounds.

Losing myself, I find him

beyond the borders of time and space.

Through the Ages, I come to know his Shining Self,

In the If of the seeker, in the voice of the poet.

Bearing so many forms, so many names,

I come down, crossing the threshold of

countless births and deaths.

The Supreme undivided, complete in himself,

embracing past and present,

Dwells in Man.

Within Him I shall find myself

The 'I' that reaches everywhere.

-Rabindranath Tagore

≈ **20** ≈

The Secret of Meditation

"As love enlivens a man's heart with pain, so ignorance teaches him the way of knowledge. Pain and ignorance lead to great joy and knowledge because the Supreme Being has created nothing vain under the Sun." — Khalil Gibran

Radha remembered what Guruji from the Ashram had told her. The technique to transcend herself: meditation. He instructed her to do meditation while living in the world and gave her the ultimate secret of meditation. It is thinking nothing. "Do not give the mind anything to play with," he had told her, "People who live within the realm of thought cannot fathom the depth of reality. The difference between a thought and the one who is aware of the thought is the difference between what is unreal and what is real."

"You need not be ascetic; you need not renounce the world. You can be — you need to be — where you are and continue to do what you are doing. Just do it with awareness; even the smallest acts of body like sitting, walking, eating, or the acts of mind like thinking, projecting, desiring, and so on. If you are angry, be totally angry. If you have to hate someone, hate totally, not in fragments. Be there hundred percent in whatever you do. This is called meditation. Then you will be able to see the beauty and the glory of your being," he had said.

Everyone had listened holding their breath. An immense silence had descended on the room. Everyone felt it in their hearts.

"Be established in your heart of consciousness. Meditation is not a movement towards anything— object or concept—but remaining conscious of yourself. It means living in an awareness of own presence, observing reality moment to moment. It is your desires only which bring you back, your craving for more finite things which prevents you from being joyful all the time. Your thoughts bind you to your mind. The moment you think anything, that object of thought draws your attention away from yourself, for you cannot be conscious of yourself—the thinker—and the thought at the same time. But when you remain in the moment of now, without even an impression of a thought, without any expectation, interpretation, or motivation, only gratitude and love, then instantly you will have the glimpse of the truth. Just as you would search for a beloved whom you have lost, search within. The Love—the Universal—will rush in as you open the gates of your heart. That will be the beginning of your quest.

"Start with where you are, what you have. Immediate reality experienced by you is your physical body connected with this physical world. You intensely identify with your body. Begin from here. It is impossible to keep your individuality inactive because action is a necessity that urges your individuality to transcend to a better state. Individuality can be transcended through individuality only. The laws of the body and mind are overcome through right perception and right action; it comes through awareness.

"When a thought arises, see from where it is arising and where it is going. When a sound is heard, see from where it arises and where it goes. When hunger comes, thirst comes, or any feeling comes, see from where it comes and where it goes. Watch it like you would watch your child playing in the park. This is meditation. Meditation gives an insight into the nature of things. It reveals that there are no such things as separate subjects and objects, as separate me and you. These are only notional conclusions of each of us from our own particular points of view—one regarding the other as the object—so that there is a vast world of objects. The affirmation of the subjectivity of all things in their proper places, to see everyone as self rather than an object is meditation. When this way of thinking matures, you will melt into the universal sea of bliss. Eventually objectless knowledge, which is real knowledge, will arise in you and burn all seeds of thought. You will emerge glorious and proud, as you are always.

"The key is: to know the basis of your being. The only person who can know you is yourself. I cannot comprehend you wholly because if I try to know you, you become an object for me and my knowledge of you will always be tainted by my likes and dislikes, judgments and opinions. If, somehow, I can know what my essence is, then it might be possible to know you since you are somewhat similar to me. By knowing one grain of sand I can know sand in its totality," he explained methodically. "You cannot have your hunger satisfied if the meal is eaten by someone else, no matter how close and intimate that person is to you. If you are hungry, you have to eat. Simple."

"How can I know myself?" Radha had asked.

"If we want to know anything, we observe that thing. Scientists of all times like Copernicus, Galileo, Newton, Einstein, and all science for that matter began with observation. They invented powerful telescopes to observe the skies, analyzed the behavior pattern of stars and planets, and their movement through the years. Galileo found out about the motion of falling bodies through observation and experimentation. Newton discovered the gravitation force through observation. Observation has magical properties. First, we observe and find consistent patterns. Then, different hypotheses are tested. If every time results are consistent, we form a conclusion. If there are any discrepancies, we try to find different conclusions. That's how we arrive at any conclusion."

"That's right."

"This is the secret of meditation. Meditation is a process to purify the mind through self-observation and self-inquiry. There is no other way. You are the most fundamental reality, undeniably and indubitably. Finding it is a scientific experiment and the only pilgrimage you have to take."

"My mind does not let me observe, so enchanted it is with the web of stories it creates." Radha remembered someone had said.

"Mind is horizontal. Just notice how it always moves from one thought to another, from the past to the future. It always moves in time. You cannot think about the present moment. You can think about the past—remembering. And you can think about the future—projecting and imagining. But how can your mind function in the present. You *can be* in the present, but you *cannot think* about the present. For thinking, space is required. And when there is no thinking, there is no mind either, only you are—the *being* that you are. It opens up a new dimension; this dimension is vertical. It falls into the depth and rises into the height. It moves in eternity—for it is without time. It is *called* Awareness."

He took a long breath, looked at everyone in the hall with welcoming warmth, and gave an infectionous smile.

"When you are totally absorbed in the present moment, then you and the world cannot exist as two. Instantly, you will get suspended in the moment of *now*. You wouldn't know if it is you who is looking at the world or you are the world. In deep presence the observer becomes the observed. The boundaries get lost, and you simply exist. You cannot find your mind in this moment, for this moment has no date or duration, knows neither before nor after. It is eternal moment. To enter deeply into it is to plunge into eternity."

Sitting there listening to the monk, Radha had felt herself so far beyond time that the past and the future melted away into obscurity. Lost in herself, transfixed by an abyss within, she touched the timeless. Everything had stood still, bursting with energy and joy.

"How can I learn this new movement, in timelessness...?"

"Time is the world; Eternity is divine. Both, human and divine, meet at a point, at the same point where any horizontal and vertical meet. It is the point of the present moment. *Stay here and now.* It is the simplest and the most natural think to do. In the beginning, not a single thought should pass by without you noticing it; notice it but without any judgment or opinion. Slowly your thoughts will become fewer and fewer, and you will begin to see the tremendous reality hiding behind it; it is self-luminous. Become free. Since your mind has been taught so many tactics, it becomes difficult for you to grasp that something so enigmatic can be so simple.

"You will begin to see that you are not different from any other person. No matter what your desires and fears are, they are within the realm of human mind. You react to everything in the world. You might be a reasonable person with a calm mind, but as soon as someone says anything about you, you react. Observe yourself as you observe any other object, without reading any meaning to it; just refuse to interpret your feelings. Then see what happens. Slowly the mist will begin to fade away and you will know yourself, truly.

"Don't ignore your fears. You have to face them: your fears, your affections, your triumphs, and your failures. If you simply watch them without any judgment, they will disappear. They are only hallucinations conjured up by your mind. You will also realize that they leave enormous energy behind; this energy is creative. Your compassion does not disappear but increase in leaps and bounds; so much that it will overwhelm you. What disappears did not exist in the first place, and what remains is all that there is—the deepest reality. This is the basic alchemy: observe and be aware, without any judgment. This is the commandment, the prayer, the burning of the candle, the ritual, the chanting of the mantra, the bowing of the head, and the singing of the hymns—the whole nine yards."

It was the first time Radha had heard such radical things. Nobody she had known in her life talked like that. It was perplexing to think that there was a transcendent presence within her. If she could just let go of her outward pursuits and sit totally empty without any thought, pure being would reveal itself in the moment of truth.

"Why, then, observation and experimentation have failed science in arriving at the reality behind the universe?" Radha had become aware of countless eyes staring at her, still bewildered at what the monk had said.

He smiled affectionately and said, "Because science is based on intellect. Intellect always dissects and analyzes. Truth is to be experienced, not analyzed. Nothing can be known by the intellect, even an atom, if it is outside. Inner growth is a different phenomenon. The whole world can use the knowledge discovered by science since the objective can be shared and taught in schools. But if you, as the point of intelligence, find the truth, it does not mean that everyone becomes enlightened. The subjective cannot be shared. You have to discover the truth through your own individual efforts. Science wants to know everything about existence, but it is ignoring its most important part: human consciousness."

"Intellect and intelligence; what's the difference?"

"The intellect always divides the whole into parts to understand a thing, whereas intelligence joins together, makes a whole out of parts. This is the greatest difference: that part exists through the whole; the whole does not exist through the part. The mystery is the whole. It is not the sum of the parts, but more than the sum.

"Let's say you find a new flower and give it to the intellect (science) to further understand it. The intellect will dissect all the elements that go into making the flower. You will know the internal structure of the flower to the minutest part, but the flower will be gone. The splendor and the wholeness of the flower would be gone. The flower was not just the sum of the parts that made the flower. It was more than the sum of the parts. When a human body is dissected for understanding human anatomy in medical schools, you can know the whole structure: lungs, kidneys, heart, but *life* that is in the living is not there. The thing that you want to understand is not there. What is the throb that was in the person before his body became a corpse? It was full of presence. Life was beating in the heart. That was intelligence, and intellect has nothing to do with it.

"Science is phenomenal; it has made very important discoveries, and it is due to science only that such astounding progress has been made in human history and is still going on, but you have to understand that this progress is external. It has made your life easier, but it has not penetrated the deeper reality. You can fly in an airplane, go from one place to another in shortest possible time through the wonders of aerodynamics, but can you be free from the bondage of gravity—that can be found out only if you go inside yourself, go inside the intelligence. Intellect is always individual; intelligence is always universal. To intellect, a person is flesh and bones. To intelligence, a person is a grand presence, a possibility. Intelligence always goes to the higher, to the pinnacle of existence. Intellect always goes to the lower.

"Science is not able to get to the bottom of the reality because every phenomenon is observed as an external something, even existence. It is not experiential. Until the time it is not experienced as a reality within, it will remain indirect knowledge imparted by teachers, religion, and scientific community. It will never become a part of you. Scientists, who have made and are still making astounding discoveries, remain subject to joy and sorrow. Knowledge is freedom, then why great scientists are not free. Conflicting emotions still rip them apart. Isaac Newton lived and died an unhappy person; Albert Einstein lived a restless life. Because they did not experience the reality as *their* reality within; it was always outside, a thing or a point in space but never themselves. I cannot quench my thirst by studying the composition of water." He had looked at the students sitting across the room, especially Radha. "It is a transcendental error. It is impossible to get an insight into anything if you don't have an insight into yourself first."

"Intellect has found out that all things in the universe are made up of tiniest strings vibrating at different levels and their essence is pure energy, but what this energy is cannot be understood unless you understand yourself first. *And* this is meditation. It is awareness. It is spontaneity. It is freedom. Whenever you understand anything, you understand through this intelligence in a flash of an experience."

Everyone had listened as if their lives depended on it, oblivious to the storm raging outside.

"The situation of the present human is like that of two friends who wanted to cross a river on a boat. The whole night they rowed the boat with all their might. They huffed and puffed until morning. When morning arrived, they realized to their amazement and disappointment that they had not moved an inch from where the boat was in the night. They were so intoxicated from the effects of liquor they had drunk at a party the previous night that they forgot to pull the anchor from the dock. The whole night was a waste of energy. Similarly, we are so intoxicated, or rather sedated, by the effects of the tempting world that we fail to use right perception and understanding. We think we have covered a great distance whereas, in reality, we have not moved an inch from where we had begun. We dig the ground and then we fill it back up. The whole of our lives we keep on doing it, thinking we have done a lot because we get defeated. If only we had the correct understanding, we would use our time in right action, leading enriching and fulfilling lives. We would make others life, too, enriching. Sadly, understanding is not there, only exhaustion."

Everyone had listened with great earnestness. Those words had profound effect on Radha.

From then on, she tried to bring her mind to the present. The endless chatter went on for some time but, finally, silence. Conscious of only breath coming in and going out, sustaining her through everything, she began to be aware of her presence. Gradually, understanding pierced her, after listening to the truth repeatedly that: from the whole came the part; from the formlessness came the form. It exhilarated her. She began to feel pleasure fill her body like water is filled in a pitcher.

The monk wanted her to understand what he was saying. There was so much self-created pain in the world. He wanted her to understand that it was all an illusion: the pain, the fear, the loneliness, the suffering, and the injustice. It was all a Phantasma; anything but reality. There were tears in his eyes to see so much pain in her eyes. She felt herself lifted by the joy of a child finding solace in mother's arms. Then she woke up.

As she closed her eyes again, she felt being pushed by some unknown force. It was a strong push. She went through few caves and tunnels, whirling and moving at infinite speed, feeling pressure building up. With a jet force she came out of the opening. Out of fear, she closed her eyes. Slowly, she opened them. Not even in her wildest dreams could she have imagined what she saw. She was in space, pure unadulterated space holding her like a mothers arm! At a distance she saw the earth with satellite circling around it. She had never seen Earth from outer space, even in pictures. It was pure peace and intense stillness. It was not an act of imagination. She was there with the aliveness of space in her, breathing with her, through her. She had become space. She was alive. It was explosive.

When she opened her eyes, space was still there at the edge somewhere. Outside, she heard a dog barking. She resisted the urge to get up. She wanted the rush of space within to persist a little longer. She closed her eyes again, enjoying every moment. She had entered the timelessness.

$$\approx 21 \approx$$

Memory

"Many a man fails to become a thinker for the sole reason that his memory is too good." —Friedrich Nietzsche

Radha was astounded to read the last two chapters of her book. She was sure she had not written such things about the Big Bang, energy, and self. She had planned to write something about it but not that profound. It didn't come from the realm of thought; it came from the heart of experience. How could Meera write all that? She was, after all, a character made by Radha. Somewhere at the edge of her mind Radha felt Meera really existed somewhere. She read and reread those pages looking for some clues to Meera's disappearance. In the end, she gave up.

She met the monk near the tree, as she took a shower. It began to happen more frequently now. First it was only in dreams after she had slept or lay down to rest, but now it began to happen anytime she was relaxed. She would find herself either near the sacred tree or the snow clad mountain. It wasn't that she resented those rendezvous, but she wanted to know the mystery. It made her restless even though she felt special to be in the middle of the mystery.

"What happened to Meera?" She asked the monk.

"You know what happened to Meera," the monk said.

"No, I don't."

"Don't be so sure."

"I am, because I don't remember writing the last two chapters when she disappeared."

"Do you remember everything you think or do? If you forget something, does that mean it didn't happen or didn't exist?"

"What are you talking about?"

"Everything is hanging upon memory," the monk said. "How do you know that you are Radha, that you have family, friends, and life, that you belong to a particular gender, city, country, and religion; because you remember yourself as such from moment to moment. From the time you are born you are a bundle of memories only. Whatever you identify with is only a memory, but a strong one that breeds identification."

Radha's attention was caught by a butterfly sucking at a flower nearby; a butterfly which was once a caterpillar. Does the butterfly remember its metamorphism from a caterpillar? She felt herself being transformed from the caterpillar to the butterfly. She cupped the butterfly in her palms, and then smiled and opened her palms towards the sky. The butterfly was still for a few moments. Then, very slowly, it spread its wings and fluttered gracefully into the air. Radha shielded her eyes against the sun and blinked as the butterfly swooped low past her face, brushing her cheeks gently with the tip of its wings. Then it rose once more into the warm air and flew into the air, growing smaller and smaller until finally it was lost from sight. As she watched it fly away, Radha's cheek began to tingle as though something was sparkling beneath her skin. She touched a hand to her face and a delicious warm feeling fizzed along her fingers, tumbling like a wave through her whole body until it reached all the way down to the tips of her toes.

"What have you got ultimately?" the monk asked seriously.

"I have my family, my friends, my education, my work." Her answer sounded false even to her, but she didn't know what else to say. She waited patiently.

He smiled, "First of all, all these relations need the support of your memory. Let's say you are hiking in the wilderness and have a nasty fall, and you wake up to realize you have lost your memory—total amnesia. You do not remember anything at all."

She knew something profound was going to come, but she was not prepared for, not even in her wildest imaginations, the question he asked then. She was left totally open and vulnerable.

"Would you have the same emotions and feeling for your children, family, and friends, then? You may pass them at a street corner without even noticing them."

"What..." was all she could utter; amazed, she stood unmoving. She never thought she could forget her children and Suraj. It was a scary thought followed by a funny feeling that the monk was right. If she didn't remember them, how would she have same feeling for them? It was an outrageous thought but a possible one. It broke her heart, and tears filled her eyes as the possibility of forgetfulness entered her mind.

"It is an upsetting thought but a possible one," she said finally with a pounding heart.

"Everything you stand for: your family, your possessions, your prestige, and your relationships with infinite things in the world— they don't really belong to you. They are totally independent of you. You can lose your property and belongings; your family and friends can change their love and affection for you. People change their views and opinions all the time. Things happen where everything can be taken, like natural calamities tsunami, hurricanes, and the like. Man made calamities like terrorist attacks can wipe away everything you believe as yours. Remember everything is placed externally in space and time, and nobody can enter into the being of another, so that nothing in the world can be possessed ultimately."

"What is real, then?"

"For something to be real, it should be real at all times and should not go under any modification or contradiction. Reality does not need any support. But there is nothing in the world which is not changing. Everything is transient. Even you are not what you were a moment ago."

Radha realized her world was fragile as a glass and yet, at times, she felt strong and powerful beyond any imagination, that she could conquer anything and everything. She wondered why such contradiction.

"What is it that I have, then?" It was breaking her heart to see that her reality was not real. She was angry at the intricate web the mind weaved.

"You can unravel the answer by reflecting on how would you know yourself if you didn't have the crutch of memory."

Radha crossed her head to indicate she didn't know.

The monk stood there calmly, regardless of the fact that Radha's world melted away, as if it didn't exist in the first place. The monk knew about its secret but not Radha.

"Use your imagination. You can look at your hands, your feet. You can touch your hair, eyes, and ears. Your perception is now different as circumstances are different. Now, due to some unforeseen event you lose your sight, hearing, and voice too. You don't have the basic sense organs to perceive the world. Now, what thoughts would go through your mind?"

"I would lose my mind too, I guess," she laughed.

"A beautiful thing will begin to happen. You will begin to live every day taking things as they come without any precepts and concepts. What you can lose does not exist in the first place. Real is what you didn't lose in such traumatic experiences."

A silent ensued which was more eloquent than any words she had ever heard. In that silence an understanding was taking place; it was a communication without speech. Their eyes met filling the space with great knowledge. Radha had a powerful insight penetrating her heart and mind. Out came a simple and profound answer, carrying her to astonishing new height.

"I existed. I didn't lose myself!"

"Yes!" the monk said excitedly, "All this time you were aware that you were. '*I know I am*' is the only truth that survives all tests and conclusions. This realization does not need the support of reason. It is spontaneous and indisputable. It defies the grasp of logical reasoning. It is a revelation rather than a conclusion."

"I have nothing to call my own, except myself!" Tears rolled down her eyes. They came as a downpour out of nowhere. She could not control them, not anymore. They were bursting out of her in all directions.

"It unravels the deepest secret of your connection with the universe. This awareness of your existence refuses to be rejected and asserts even before you begin to think. What is left after everything else is gone is you, not Radha, but being; not a person, but an aware existence. For

Radha to exist, she needs her relations and memories to identify with. It is the fundamental 'I' always existing in the background, at the core, untouched and pure, all brilliance and light. Everything crumbles in front of I. *And you are that.*" There were tears in his eyes, tears of joy and compassion.

Extraordinary things were happening, she felt it within; such joy, but she was still unable to grasp it fully. How could she be the purest and the grandest? Such magnificence and, still, she liked to cling to the finitude. If a butterfly told the caterpillar it could fly, would it believe the butterfly?

But Radha forgot one thing. Truth is stronger than false; real is stronger than unreal. She was still recouping from the effect of true knowledge, her mind staggering like a ten-month-old learning to walk.

"Well, suppose there is a fire in your house. What would be your reflex, what would be the most precious thing you would save? It is hard question to answer but a very profound one."

"Any person inside the house rather than anything else," Radha replied.

"Let's say the fire is spreading, and it is dangerous to enter the house. Now what would you do?"

"I don't know. Look for help, pray..." Her voice broke off as another truth began to dawn on her.

"You will be overtaken by sadness at your inability to help but no matter how dear the person inside the house is, you will save your life first."

Radha thought of a dear friend who was in a car accident. She was driving her daughter to her school. Both of them survived with no injuries. She told Radha later that at the time of the accident, for some moments, she actually forgot about her daughter, so scared she was about getting hurt herself. Later on she was consumed with guilt on forgetting her child.

The monk had an intense expression on his face as he spoke, "This is not selfishness. This self love is holy. It stands at the topmost, most precious, glorious, and the grandest of everything; it is above the wealth and beyond the relations with the world. It is predominant in everyone. Even the most miserable person asking for death would not like to die when death really comes knocking on the door. Even if everything goes, let me be alive at least. And this is love.

"It is glory that breathes with you, sees with you, hears with you, thinks with you. Beyond the comprehension of human mind, it stands as the eternal subject. It resides in the heart of every being. Everyone knows the world as 'I', not as 'you' or 'this'. Everyone is a subject rather than an object. Everything is filled with utter subjectivity. It is absolute awareness where you are not aware of your individual personality, but you are not unaware of anything."

Radha was too stunned to think. And then, the mist began to lift, and things began to make sense, and she began to think aloud: "No matter where I am, whatever my loves and hates are, these are details. Even if I move with the speed of light where time stops, 'I' is already there. It is the only constant in this world as well as in any other world because 'I' comes first, experience comes later. There is no other way to exist."

Radha was surprised by her voice. She listened attentively as if she was listening to someone else and, at the same time, was raised to wondrous heights.

"I want to listen more," Radha said.

The monk said, "It—the unbroken 'I' consciousness—is the original principle behind every thought and understanding. We are always embraced by divine in all our thoughts and actions. It transcends all phenomenons since it is being, not becoming. While becoming has a tendency to move towards the external, being is a withdrawal into the depths within. Waves can be said to be individual 'I''s and the ocean the universal 'I'. No matter how many waves there are, the ocean is still the same."

Radha found herself being carried away by his words. It was having an infectious effect on her. The Monk was looking at her in the most affectionate way. Had she reached heaven, Radha wondered again. She observed herself from the top of the head to the bottom of the toes, in reverence. Gratitude filled her as she spoke, "Behind this beautiful structure of my body and mind is the pinnacle of truth—I myself as pure subjectivity, the experiencer as well as the experience! I am existence, I am eternity!"

≈ **22** ≈

The Fiction of Death

"For what is to die but to stand naked in the wind and to melt into the Sun? And what is it to cease breathing but to free the breath from its restless tides, that it may rise and expand and seek god unencumbered?" — Khalil Gibran

"Do you ever remember the time when you did not exist?"

The question sent Radha gasping in her mind. Before she could think, another question came, "Where were you before you were born, and where will you go when you die?" the monk asked.

Radha thought hard.

He was looking at her tenderly. "Let's say, you were in a fatal accident and lying on a hospital bed. You have an hour before you die. Everything is beyond your control, and in that moment you can do two things. Either you can hold on and become miserable, or you can surrender and let go. You look at your family and friends gathered around to bid their farewells. You are worried about your children but have lost the capacity to take control of the situation. You reflect on your life, achievements, and defeats, and try not to hold on to that because in few minutes you would be gone. You realize that eventually nothing belongs to you, even your physical body to which you cling so much. You are drifting into a sleep that is getting sweeter and sweeter every moment. Finally, you fall into a deep, refreshing sleep which is normally called death."

Fear gripped Radha. It was not a nice feeling, to think of one's mortality. She was a mother, a spouse, a friend. She had responsibilities. But she realized it was not a distant possibility; it could happen any time. She could be in an accident. She remembered when a tsunami took hundreds of thousands of lives a few years ago. Death was everywhere with its immense force. It did not discriminate. It did not care whether one was rich or poor, good or bad. It just claimed whoever came into its path. What was the power she, as a human, had when she could not escape death; it was beyond anyone's control. She realized she could run away from, argue with, or deny life, but death was final. There was no argument. Once it came, it came—naked and intense, proud and glorious.

She was shaken to her core. With all her intellectual dialogue and seeking, nature could crush her any time and melt her into nothingness. *'Would I cease to exist then?'* Then a strange thing happened. As Radha was contemplating that she might die, she realized it did not make sense. She could imagine horrible things happening to her but not to exist...that was not possible. Every day she saw people die, but she refused to accept that she could be annihilated.

"I cannot shake this feeling of being here forever, even if not in present life and circumstances," she finally burst out.

"Be careful. This is a powerful statement," the monk cautioned her.

"I might die in a physical sense, but I cannot cease to exist. No one can cease to exist." She was surprised at the strength of her own doubtlessness.

A silence followed that was strangely alive. It had no origin, and the whole existence was part of it.

"Today you have become fearless. As long as you are scared of something, it takes hold of you. As soon as you embrace what you are scared of, it lets you go. You become fearless," the monk declared.

"Just think where you were before you were born? Did your existence begin the day you were born in this present life, and will it end the day you die?" he asked intensely.

"No. Something is gravely wrong with this kind of thinking. This does not make sense. I feel I have always been here, even before time began. Why do I feel like that?" she asked through the tears rolling down her eyes.

"Because you are ancient! Because you are eternal! You will always be here, forever and ever. Even though forgetfulness has overtaken your mind, reality remains the same, except you don't remember it. That you cease to exist when you die is heresy."

After a slight pause he asked further, "How old is Earth?"

"I think scientists are calculating it to be 400 billion years old," Radha remembered from a documentary she watched on television.

"You have to see yourself not only from the infinity of space, but also from the eternity of time. For 100 billion years there was nothing but volcanic eruptions. Then, only water life was there. Gradually, as gases escaped from Earth, an ozone layer was formed and some water creatures began to crawl on land. The dinosaurs came and lived for billion years. Something destroyed them, maybe a huge meteorite, and after the dust settled, different animals came. It does not matter what came first, but where were you when there was only water life or dinosaurs or volcanoes?"

Radha looked at the monk as if she was looking at something amazing.

"Don't you see—you existed as the wetness in water, the greenness in trees. You existed in the heat of volcanoes, in the breath of winds, in the warmth of fire, and in the flight of wings. You existed in the solidity of the mountains, in the fluidity of liquids, in the melody of songs. You are the beauty in beautiful, the formlessness in form, and the unmanifest in manifest. Just as you see only that which is within the visible spectrum of light, you don't see that your existence extends beyond your knowledge. It is immeasurable. You are ancient and eternal, for you are existence!" He was unable to contain the excitement rising within and began to dance.

"After you die physically, you become conscious of yourself again, in a womb getting ready to be re-born. You are then a baby. You do not remember your past life, your attachments and fears, your joys and sorrows. You have new set of people and situations, new set of ambitions and grudges. Just because you don't remember your past life does not mean it did not happen. When you exit from the present life, you fall into a forgetfulness and are remade again and again, millions of time, for ages and ages. Just like when you wake up from sleep. If every day you forget your continuity on waking up, then everyday you would be born, and every day you would die. The difference between death and sleep is that in sleep you wake up to the same life, and in death you wake up to a new life."

Radha stood there, frozen in time.

"If you can stretch your imagination and think what it was like to be born, imagine yourself existing in the womb of a mother, simply existing with no thoughts or ideas. Now, you are a new born, then a-year-old, five-years-old. When you grow up, you don't remember all the things you have experienced; still, you are a product of all those moments. All human knowledge proceeds out of experience. No one remembers their early childhood, and if existence depends upon memory, then no one has existed as babies. It is simply gossip that something didn't happen because we don't remember it."

"Why I don't remember the continuity when I wake up to a new life after death?"

"Think of it as a kind of defense mechanism installed by nature for your own good, for human evolution. If you remembered all your previous births, it would be utter chaos. How would you create, express, and experience? So many times you feel déjà vu, a feeling of familiarity. These are little remembrances which have been hidden in your unconscious mind. You rejoice at birth and shed tears at death, but fail to realize that the death of a caterpillar is the birth of a butterfly. Everyone is evolving into a better state due to this phenomenon of death and life working uniformly in the cosmos."

"Who or what decides the kind of life I would live in the next birth?"

"Remember, you will not be taken to a place you have not thought of or desired. Your unfulfilled longings will take you to the place where it can find fulfillment. Your strong thoughts in the present will decide your future life."

"What about destiny?"

"Destiny is nothing but the other side of free will. We tend to blame others for our faults and misfortunes—or we conjure up a ghost and call it fate. We don't want to see that we are the powerful creators of our own fate. It is too much of responsibility. We make your own destiny. The sun shines for the weak as well as for the strong. Infinite power is open to us, at all times, in all places, under all conditions. It is up to us how we use it. We have to take responsibility for our own choices and actions. The future is before us as a potentiality. Always remember that each word, thought, and choice has the power to make us or break us.

"We have been born countless times, we have died countless times. We have been a father, a mother, a beloved, a friend, an enemy, a king, a criminal countless times. There is no such thing called a stranger. Millions of times we were on the topmost crest of the wave, and million times we were down at the bottom of despair."

She heard in words what she had always known in her thoughts. They broke the boundary she had created around herself, the boundary of the reality of present life and everything included in it.

Radha looked intently in the eyes of the monk, her mind utterly still. Slowly, there rose explosive energy that carried her to that which was beyond all measure.

≈ 23 ≈

Different Dimensions

"In the deepest recess of our heart there is a great secret of Creation. The miracles of Eternity and Infinity are hidden within." — Swamiji

The morning was heavy with fog. It hid everything: the grandeur of the mountains, the strength of the trees, and the expanse of the sky. It had beauty of its own, moving without a direction or motivation. Birds were silent, so was the lush green vegetation, and yet they spoke more eloquently than with words. Every little thing was intensely alive with beauty. Radha saw a leaf and it was the leaf of every tree and bush. She listened to a sound and it was the voice of existence.

Gradually, the sun began to rise and with it came light, light that entered into the deep corners that were hidden before. It was lighting the fringes of her thought, giving a passing delight. It exposed Radha's heart and mind if she allowed it. She had a feeling if she let it, it would enter into the unexplored regions of her mind where she had hovered around the edges but never been. She had to be ready, for then she would be open and vulnerable without any hiding place; no thoughts and ideas to cling to.

She heard a bird at a distance. It had depth. In that stillness, the sound was pure. She realized she could understand the bird's song and its delight. There was a deep presence in the background. Silence persisted, and with every slightest sound her depths exploded. It was not even an experience, because in every experience she was there as an experiencer, separate from the object and the act of experience. But there was none. She had become sound.

She realized that a mind caught in thought could never grasp it. The complete stillness of mind—is not a thing to be comprehended or analyzed. It is a *being* that can only be experienced when all thoughts and even the memory of thoughts cease. It's an extraordinary thing, not inertia, but one filled with the stillness of within. After a while, she drifted into sleep and found herself on the snow clad mountains. Both, the monk and the woman were there. Radha somehow knew the time had come and she was ready.

"Who are you?"

"We are part of your consciousness," the pair said in unison.

"Then how can you give me so much knowledge I didn't know earlier?"

"You may appear to be a separate individual coming from a particular family and country, but underneath you are connected to all. In a cosmic magic act, one appears to be many. Water may erroneously identify with separate waves, but it is the same continuum of the ocean. There is no separation, no barrier, except that of an imaginary one conjured up by mistaken identification. You have complete knowledge at all times, but it remains hidden due to your identification with your physical body," the monk said with excitement. "Whatever you want to know and wish to experience, you can, right here and now, by accessing that part of consciousness. There are no hindrances whatsoever. Since you are so caught up in the affairs of the world, you fail to recognize and acknowledge such abundance.

"When you go deep within and sink into the abyss of unknown—beyond the mind and away from the hindrances of thoughts, you will recognize at once the substantiality of your nature with the nature of the world and everything in between. You will enter the universe, for entering into your own being is identical to entering into everybody's being. There is no reality independent of consciousness. And consciousness is indivisible. World is not unreal. But it is not absolute either. When the need to experience arises, simultaneously, the world arises. You are an individual wave in the ocean of experiences. You are *consciousness,* I am *consciousness,* and whatever exists in between us is *consciousness.*"

"Why, then, do I experience space, time, and matter?" Radha asked.

"It is just like as you dream," the woman said.

"A dream,"

"[4]The phenomenon through which you dream is the same phenomenon through which you experience the world. You have to explore the dynamics of dreaming, waking, and sleeping dimensions. Which one is real?" the woman asked.

"Definitely, waking," replied Radha.

"It is only your interpretation. Stop for a moment and think and understand that all are states of existence; different states, but states nevertheless. These are only different dimensions you cover in a day."

"Dreams are just dreams; there is no foundation behind them. Everyone lives in the same waking world while everyone's dream world is different. What kind of mystery is this?" Radha asked.

"It is such an interesting phenomenon that happens every day, and we never raise a question. Ask yourself, are you the same person who is awake as the one who is dreaming?"

"Yes, I am," Radha said with confidence.

"Don't be so quick in answering. It will be true if you exist in both the states simultaneously. But you don't; continuously, yes, but not simultaneously. You are talking from the waking consciousness point of view. You don't pass such judgment while you were in a dream, because, then, you were not aware of being in a dream," the monk said.

Both of them were looking intensely at Radha.

"That's right, now that I think about it," Radha said, deep in thought.

"When you are awake, you identify with waking consciousness. When you are dreaming, you identify with dreaming consciousness," the woman clarified.

"But when I dream, it is me who is dreaming," Radha said puzzled.

"Your statement is self contradictory because when one is, other is not. Waking mind and dreaming consciousness cannot exist simulta-

---

[4] Inspired by ancient Hindu text Mandukya Upanisad.

neously. This slipping into a dream is so swift that you are not there to know that the event has taken place. It is like magic which defies any logic."

"Waking and dreaming consciousnesses are separate, I think I am beginning to understand. This opens a new way of thinking. Pioneers in the field of dreams say that we dream our most suppressed thoughts."

The monk spoke patiently, "The relevant question is not what you dream, but how you dream. There is a dreaming individuality within you, forcing your mind to undergo intense modification, creating a situation of apparent spatial temporal world of dream similar to the one in waking dimension; it is the same mind which has divided itself into the subject and the object, the seer and the seen. What matters is that you are able to create a world of externality similar to the waking world and call it the dream world. The entire world of perception is involved in the world of the perceiver. Things seen and felt in dreams do not exist at all. They are 'you' only."

"I am the beholder of the dream, and also the dream," Radha muttered to herself.

"The same is true about the waking world. You are the beholder of the world, and you *are* the world! This is the secret. The entire structure of your existence is hidden in this relationship between dreaming and waking dimensions. If you can unlock this secret, you have unlocked the secret of creation. You neither belong to the waking nor to the dreaming dimension. Waking and dreaming experiences cannot exhaust you; neither can they comprehend your being. You are an awareness that observes. There exists an ability within you that transcends particulars of both, and stands above as an observer."

Radha tried to speak but nothing came out of her mouth.

"If dreaming world is an effect of and created from the impressions of the waking world, then waking world is also an effect of and created from the impressions of some other higher world. *And* you would not know which, until you wake up to such higher consciousness," the monk spoke.

Radha began to feel dizzy. Everything around her was turning into an unreality so real that she could touch it.

"If a comparison of two states is responsible for regarding the dream world as unreal, why do you not make a similar comparison with another higher state? Why do you confine the analysis to these two states only?" the woman questioned.

"Because I don't see or experience a higher state, if there is one," Radha replied.

The woman spoke, "You are a magician under the spell of your own magic—of the belief in the reality of waking life. You are oblivious of there being such a thing as waking life when you are wrapped up in your dream. In the same way, you are so bewitched with the waking life, so charmed by the mesmerizing show going on that you remain oblivious of the existence of such a thing as higher dimension. You have to undo the spell. You have to acknowledge and embrace, humorously and wholeheartedly, the fact that you are under the spell, and then only you can undo it. Then see the joy of living."

"Why does everyone live in the same waking world but have different dream worlds?" Radha asked.

This time the monk spoke, "In this tiny space between us there are millions of different worlds, but since you live on a certain level of reality and them on others, you cannot comprehend them, therefore cannot acknowledge them. They are there in plain sight, just like various frequencies in the air. All people living in the same waking world are on the same level of reality. Remember: the frequency, constitution, and density of your psychic apparatus."

"Suppose you are dreaming that you were a king ruling over the whole world. You are not sad on waking up that you lost your dream wealth. Why?" the woman asked.

A smile crossed Radha's lips. "It is not real."

"Observe the subtlety of your statement. No matter how pleasant the dream was, you wake up as a whole individual. You don't leave the dream world somewhere at some point in time and space, but dissolve it instantly into waking consciousness. Subjectivity in the waking dimension is of higher reality than the one in dreaming dimension. But is there a reality higher than the reality experienced in waking?" the monk asked

Radha replied, "There are times when I find myself in reflections giving suggestions of higher realities: when I stand at the edge of the ocean and look at the vast expanse that there is, when I climb to the peak of a mountain and look at the creation spread everywhere, when I look in the eyes of a child, when I smile at a stranger, when I see flowers bloom, butterflies flutter, seasons change, I feel and know and experience that there is higher dimension. In random acts of kindness and compassion, in all acts of spontaneity, I have experienced the dimension beyond this world."

"Naturally this higher dimension should be inclusive of all lower ones including the waking dimension," the woman said. "The higher dimension is included in you, just like dreaming individual is included in you. Reality is only as far away from you as your waking mind is from your dreaming one. The distance is not in space or time, but in perception. The world of space, time, and matter might just be a perception of the universal mind. How a thought can externalize itself into an apparent space-time complex, creating a world of so called solidity is demonstrated in everyday dream experiences. If your individual mind can create a dream world, then the transcendental mind can create this world."

Radha felt she was standing at the edge of eternity. How do I dream, what's the process?" she asked.

"Do not ask such questions, or it will shake the very foundation on which you are standing," the woman said.

"I am made of such stuff as dreams are made of—just like Shakespeare had said," Radha muttered.

"Infinity is hidden in every grain of sand. The seed of universal powers are hidden in your own individual cells," the woman said in a finale.

Radha heard some voices. She opened her eyes. Abhi and Anya were standing at the foot of the bed laughing and playing. For a moment she forgot who or where she was. Then, she remembered everything—was she dreaming now or was she dreaming then? She looked tenderly at Abhi and Anya, and she looked at the tree outside the front window of her room—were they the same as her? Her mind went numb thinking about the dynamics of dreaming and waking dimension.

Radha kept thinking about the waking and dreaming dimension the entire day. She picked a pebble from the sidewalk and kept it at her writing table. She looked at it whenever she could, wondering if she created the pebble as she creates her dreams.

She waited patiently as the night approached and went to bed early, full of anticipation.

She asked her next question as she saw the monk. "How do I get to know the observer, the one who is supposed to be me only?"

"Where do you go when you go to sleep? Where are you when you are dreaming? Reflect on that. You will get to the witness," he answered. "The key is hidden in the structure of sleep, if only you can keep yourself from the wonderful intoxication the mind offers. There is complete cessation of the activities of your mind. It doesn't matter if you are a genius or dumb, good or evil. You become one homogeneous mass of consciousness and nothing is projected outside. [5]Now the perplexing question is: if you don't have any external consciousness, how do you know you exist in sleep."

The question intrigued her. It was the most logical question she was ever been faced with.

"Because I have a memory of having slept," she answered.

"Memory is a remembrance of an experience. You cannot remember anything that you have not experienced. Even though there is no consciousness in sleep, somehow, your existence seems to be asserted since you the same person as you were before you slept. This link of continuity cannot be an unconscious one. Even to make an assertion that it was darkness, there must be knowledge of darkness," he said.

Radha was getting more and more intrigued.

"Not only this," the monk pointed out further, "but the pleasure of sleep is better than any other pleasure of waking life. How refreshing and energizing it is to wake up from sleep. The worst of sorrows and

---

[5] Inspired by ancient Hindu text, Mandukya Upanisads.

moments of profound happiness become absent. There are no grudges, you ask for nothing, nobody to see or talk to, and you are happier in sleep than in any other condition—totally unprotected and unseen, without any possessions and relationships."

"From where is all this happiness coming?" Radha asked.

"You touch the foundation of your being in sleep. And it is full of bliss," the monk replied. "A profound phenomenon is happening giving such total delight that you want nothing else. Just as it is separate from dreaming and waking, it is also separate from sleeping consciousness. Everything is negated except your existence. It is the point from where awareness arises, thoughts, feelings, and understanding arises, mind arises, senses arise, ego arises. You don't know who this deepest self is. You know who the deepest self is not. It is not your body, not your senses, not your mind."

"If am not Radha then who am I, or rather what am I?"

"You are transcendental! You are pure, eternal, and blissful—for you are Consciousness! It is impossible to exist as anything else. A strong veil of mind prevents you from experiencing as such. Otherwise, you wouldn't know you exist in sleep. You are the knower of yourself, and knower cannot be unconscious at any time. The same consciousness persists for ages together, for eons and eons. It is endless. An experience of deep sleep, pure and simple, is unlocking the secret of being."

"I exist as pure being in sleep!" Radha felt she was the only person in the cosmos, and the entire cosmos loved her totally.

The monk was smiling. "Once in a jungle, a lion gave birth to a cub and died. A herd of sheep was nearby, and they raised the cub as their own. The cub grew up thinking him to be sheep. Then one day another lion was passing by and saw the cub, and he was surprised to see him behaving like sheep. The cub looked at him as if he were a stranger. The lion tried to explain that he was a lion too, but cub just looked at him suspiciously. Finally, the lion took the cub to a river and showed him his face. The lion roared and showed the cub that he could roar too. As the cub roared, he became aware of his true identity as a lion. In a flash, he became aware that he was a lion, that he was never a sheep."

Everyone became silent for a moment.

"This is what has happened to all of us," he continued. "We are suffering from mistaken identities. We believe we are what we are not—and believe it so strongly that we close the possibility of thinking that we can be complete and perfect, that our being is intrinsically valid by its own existence, that we are made of awareness extending into the infinitude of experience that transcends space-time."

Radha felt exhilarated. "What can I do to undo the mistaken identity?"

The monk said with authority, "You just have to reshuffle our consciousness. In a dream you may think you are a bird or an animal. To know your real identity, you don't have to move in space or time but adjust your consciousness then and there. As soon as realization dawns about your truth, in this case waking up, everything falls into place. That's all."

The woman said," Enjoy the spell, but shift the perception. Acknowledge the love, and embrace the joy. Life is a delight; enjoy it to the fullest. And only you can do it. No one else can do it for you."

It was the middle of the night. Everything had gone still. Radha's mind had become utterly quite. Her body also lay there on the bed motionless. She could hear the movement of silence, moving in itself. There was no past or future, only the vast space of now. It was the purity of everything there was. The purity rushed in Radha's heart; it overwhelmed her as tears of joy rolled down her cheeks.

≈ **24** ≈

The Final Dialogue

"No man can reveal to you aught but that which already lies half asleep in the dawning of our knowledge. If he is indeed wise he does not bid you enter the house of wisdom, but rather leads you to the threshold of your own mind. The astronomer may speak to you of his understanding of space, but he cannot give you his understanding. The musician may sing to you of the rhythm which is in all space, but he cannot give you the ear which arrests the rhythm nor the voice that echoes it." —Khalil Gibran

When Radha woke up the next day it seemed the time had stopped. The morning stood deep with the night. The night had made it richer, made it alive with an intensity that was fragile in its purity. It was a beautiful morning, bringing joy that only glory brings.

Radha looked at the sacred tree. It was a magnificent tree, splendid in its hugeness. She sat under its welcoming shade and wondered, was she watching the tree or she was the one been watched. For a split second she felt there was no dividing line between her, the tree, and the birds; it was one life beating in all hearts. There was only love, but the mind, so active with knowledge and experience, was not aware of such sweeping beauty.

"Who are you?" Radha asked the monk one last time.

His eyes motioned her to turn and look behind. A number of trees, birds, and people had mysteriously appeared behind her. People she had met and known in her life: her parents, Suraj, Abhi, Anya, Anita, Shalini, countless other people whom she didn't remember, people she hadn't thought of in a long time, her fourth grade teacher with whom she never got along, that friend from high school with whom she had a falling out, even strangers with whom she'd had a chance meeting— hundreds of them. As she asked the question the monk's face transformed into her face. He had a smile that was at once secretive and revealing. It was him but with her face. She turned and looked at hundreds of people, all of their faces transformed into her face. She saw the transformation. Before she could think—all the trees and birds, each and every blade of grass, every pebble on the ground transformed into her. Her mind staggered at the bewildering fact that everyone was her!

She opened her eyes and came back to the waking state.

She closed her eyes and came to the dreaming state.

She knew it was not a dreaming state since she could not be dreaming and awake at the same time. She was in some other dimension. She had expanded and had become the one that existed in space! The world existed within her, literally. There was no without. There was only one single screen where layers of depth were experienced. *And* she was the screen. She woke up exploding in bliss.

"Where am I?"

"You are at the same point where you have always been. The point has expanded and has become space. It is the point of the Big Bang, and it is the same as your being. You do not live in the universe, the universe lives in you," the woman said in the same loving voice.

In a flash, Radha saw that she was in her room only.

She was in her room and also inside the hollow space of the tree.

Both existed at the same place!

Then she realized that the snow clad mountain was also at the same place!

The monk was smiling at her. The woman was smiling at her.

The monk said, "Multiple dimensions exist within the same space. A thin veil prevents you from experiencing all the worlds at the same time. It is for your own best. In the space of this room, you are surrounded by radio waves, electromagnetic fields, and various frequencies. Imagine, if somehow you can open all the channels of the television at the same time. Nothing would make sense, and you would go mad."

"Then why did I begin to experience these multiple levels?"

"Because of your awakening, your persistence to know the truth. Reality is self luminous. Truth is hidden under dust. When you emptied your mind of thoughts, Truth rushed in and you began to perceive other dimensions, not as a favor but as a natural consequence. You began to see the real. The toys of the world ceased to distract you, and you saw the mother standing next to you, always standing by you."

"I don't perceive it clearly."

"Because there still exists some doubts, fears, and desires in your mind. When all doubts will disappear, you will see the reality as clear as water, and then you will stand glorious in your own splendor."

"[6]A story will explain the mystery of multiple dimensions. In ancient times, there lived a king and his queen. He had a huge kingdom and the queen loved him immensely, but she always worried about his life. She prayed and meditated for a long time. She was bestowed a blessing that if the king died he would never leave the room that they both shared. It so happened, in a battle, the king died. Queen was overcome by grief. She asked God about her blessing. An angel appeared and told her that the king was in the same room. She couldn't see him because it was a whole other dimension, and she and her senses lived in another. To pacify her, the angel gave her divine vision for the time being, so that she could travel between space and time, and see for herself the reality. She saw that the king was an eighteen year old prince of a vaster kingdom than what he had before. The entire kingdom was contained in the space of one room. Queen asked the angel—how was it possible. The kingdom contained space vaster than the room and the king had died three days ago. How could he be reborn and have lived eighteen years of his life in a span of three days.

"The angel smiled and told her that that was not all. She told her the secret of her past life. She and the king were ordinary people who lived modestly. One day, there arose an intense desire in their minds to be king and queen, on seeing the procession of the king of the country they lived in. Since the situation in their life at that time was not conducive to that, when they died they were reborn as king and queen.

---

[6] Inspired by ancient Hindu text Yoga Vasistha.

Unable to believe the story, the queen asked for proof. The angel again gave her divine vision so that she could travel through time and space, and she saw that an old couple, who were she and her husband, had died and their children were mourning them. They had died eight days ago! She was perplexed; how could they have died eight days ago in another dimension *and* be born and have lived a long, happy life as king and queen, only to have the king die again and be reborn as a prince, who had already lived eighteen years in yet another dimension. And all in a span of three days and within the space of one room! The angel clarified that it all sounded incredible, but the vast kingdom was only in the house of an ordinary person on account of his intense desire for a kingdom. The memory of the past is hidden, and death is but waking from a dream."

Trying to grasp the phenomenal truth, Radha went deep into herself. "What was my past life and what will be the next?"

"Why does it matter when the birth that rises from a wish is no more real than the wish, like waves in a mirage. At every point there are worlds within the worlds." the monk laughed.

"Take the example of a movie. No real people are moving on the screen, but they are projected from thin films moving at rapid speed so that it gives the illusion of moving people and things. You know you are watching a movie, but still so many times you get so engrossed that you forget it is a movie and begin to identify with the characters and experience real emotions. You know now—thanks to scientific discoveries—that there are nothing called trees, rivers, galaxies, and people, but everything as energy vibrating at infinite speed. Its movement at a certain speed gives the apparition of trees, rivers, galaxies, people as such. It is all space—which is aware and capable of thought; it is holy space."

"How can space think and experience?"

"Has the question occurred to you how can you think and experience, or why water is wet or fire hot. Experience is inherent in Consciousness. When it expands, it becomes space and undergoes through the fields of various experiences."

"Why it is not apparent to the eye?"

"Because you see the world as matter, not as energy. The day you begin to see people not as mother, father, friend, or stranger but as living energy; trees, mountains, rivers, galaxies as grand presence, then your perception will change effortlessly and a new world will emerge, the real world. Just as you see wood in all trees, water in all ripples; similarly, you have to see vibrant energy in all names and forms. When you see a tree you become aware of it as tree due to ages and eons of conditioning. Now you have to decondition everything and start to see everything as a continuum of conscious energy, full of laughter and joy. When this thinking matures, the veil of mind will melt in the fire of knowledge, and you will see the reality as it is, not as you want it to be.

"If space-time complex is the fabric of the cosmos, then it can be ripped by hammering any point on it with attention. A hole can be made at any point through persistent awareness, and then see the magic happen. It carries immense force—attention. The point will show its real identity, and it will also reveal the reality hidden behind. You can travel anywhere, anytime, in any space, and in any time. Science is trying to create time machines, find portals, or create them—gateways to different realities. All that is needed is attention, an awareness of your own presence, then the limitation of space-time will cease to operate for your mind, for space-time is also a kind of mind only."

A shiver went down her spine.

She woke up feeling a sense of well-being—that everything was well with the world. Immense gratitude filled her for being at the right place, for being alive. The world was a beautiful place, and she was blessed to be the part of it. There was nothing else she could do, would want to do, except just be.

≈ **25** ≈

The Final Meditation

Who is this...

Who lives in my innermost being; has been with me through ages.

Who sees through my eyes; speaks through my voice; hears through my ears; thinks through my mind.

Whose hidden touches have made me sublime.

He tells me I am a wonder; He tells me to behold myself in all my glory and splendor.

These glorious mountains, these majestic trees, this awe inspiring universe exists for me.

He shakes me from my slumber and asks me to behold all the beauty there is.

I look at him with doubt; I am intoxicated with the world and its riches; world of temptation holds so much promise.

I ignore him, I lose him.

The world with its grandeur entices me no more.

Like a lost love I long for him.

I go to temple, I go to church. He is nowhere to be found.

I am tired. I give up.

Behold, there he is. My whole being is exploding with joy.

He never left me. He was where I was.

I just never saw him.

Every day I meditate, every day I contemplate on the simple, deeper truths of the universe. Every day I observe myself objectively, and every day I become more and more aware. Gradually, layers around me have begun to peel off, one by one. I have begun to see the stories I have woven around myself, my defense mechanisms, the way I relate to others and the way I assert my individuality; the way I act and react in the given environment, and the way others around me act and react to each other. Nothing is happening, but since I believe in the reality of things I react to them. Once I am stripped of my stories, judgments, and interpretations I have nothing to hang on to. I begin see a totally new dimension I was unaware before, but which exists always.

What is in me is in everyone. The stuff I am made of is the same stuff everyone else is made of—it is the stuff of reality. As I observe myself pleasure begins to fill my being. This observation is different from looking at me in a mirror as an object. This observation is being aware of a point within, acting as the center of awareness that I exist. It is from here all thoughts, feelings, and understandings arise. It is magical how such a simple thing as being aware of my own presence is the answer to all the questions. It overwhelms me. Spontaneously, I sing and dance. Thoughts pour on me at the same time inspiring me. Words come out of my mouth arranged in a poetic form. Tears of joy overtake me on seeing simple things, like flowers, trees, birds, sun, moon, stars, and winds rustling through the air. I meditate some more and waves of goodness overtake me. All complaints from life fade away in forgetfulness. My stories have become like a childhood memory. All I desire now is to be here in this bliss forever and ever.

Strikingly astounding knowledge comes as I contemplate. I hear a sound—any sound and I wonder, how does it arise and how does it subside. It could be a melody or noise; it still comes from within the realm of sound. It dawns on me that sound comes from within me. When birds sing, when thunderclouds roar, when the wind blows, something inside me also stirs. The acts of hearing, the objects making sound and I are not three different things but a single whole. I get goose bumps. I have become sound.

When the sun rises in the sky, it also rises in me. When the moon adorns the night, it adorns me too. I look at myself and I look at everything around me. Form and formlessness both are aspects of reality. The unmanifest is invisible and the manifest is visible. My form and body is visible but the fundamental essence behind me is not. As I look at objects around me—the bed, the walls, the tree outside the room—they start to lose their solidity and merge with me. Waves of bliss rush in and astound me with an unknown force. It becomes hard to distinguish if I am observing the objects or I am the one being observed. All distinctions disappear and one expanse remains; it is filled with completeness. Something so enigmatic and splendid can be so simple to be had in an instant anywhere, anytime. The rest are details. Truth is only this much.

There arises within me such love and compassion for each and everything that has ever existed—because they are me only. As I walk, I do not know if I am walking outside or inside myself. I have become the cosmos. My real identity has taken me into its bosom and I explode with infinite bliss. It is called the bliss of being.

Meera
Written by: Radha

≈ 3 ≈

The Point of the Big Bang

"A human being is part of the whole, called by us 'Universe, a part limited in time and space. He experiences himself, his thoughts and feelings as something separated from the rest- a kind of optical delusion of his consciousness. This delusion is a kind of prison for us, restricting us to our personal desires and affection for a few persons nearest us. Our task must be to free ourselves from this prison by widening our circle of compassion to embrace all living creatures and the whole nature in its beauty." —Albert Einstein

Meera wrote to clear her head, but there were times when she was convinced that the thoughts were coming from her but they were not hers. She would be inspired by them. She could not negate the moments of heightened alertness, in the absence of thoughts, when her mind became utterly silent and everything came alive. At those times, she found her presence spread from within to everywhere: the sun, the moon, and the stars. She would enter the timelessness, and experience enhanced peace and completeness. It was only in that immeasurable silence she would experience the flashes of the immense. She would stand redundant in front of it.

It was in those moments as the splendor surrounded her that she wrote about the Big Bang:

The Big Bang started at a point which expanded into the universe, a universe so vast and immense in proportion that it instills fear as well as reverence in our minds. It is from here the mystery began. It is the point which is outside the boundaries of intellect, but it is the nucleus of our ever-expanding universe.

It cannot be a point in space and time, because space was created by the Big Bang. Both space and time coexist. Then I am sitting at the same point from where it—the beginning of creation—began, and no time has elapsed since time did not exist. That means creation has not taken place at all. It has just been projected. I am at the same place and time I have always been!

Just a slight shift in perception is needed to see that it (the point) is the intelligent living force of the universe. Within the space of a single point I exist, I create, I experience. It exists in me and it exists in you. It exists everywhere. Nothing is outside it but includes within itself everything, even eternity. As it became aware of itself, it began to experience and Creation took place. Just as fluidity is inherent in liquid, experience is inherent in this eternal point, which, when stirs with notions becomes the mind. Oh, what glory! Look at the splendor. My whole being has become the point. Existence resides in it.

Meera's face was glowing with happiness at having found something which was lost. Her face had taken on the aura of an unknown brilliance, so absorbed in thinking beyond thought that it took precedence over everything else. She was filled with an unusual energy.

If the universe is projected, then who is projecting it? How is such vast a space as the universe is experienced within the space of a point?

In a flash, it came, and then it was gone—epiphany at a powerful, random moment:

When I dream or when I think, I experience space but there is no actual space, only my mind experiencing space. Subjectivity within me expands without any external reality. How little I know and how intellectual I feel. My ego's work is accomplished. It has seduced me completely. The truth is beyond me, greater than my personality, but also belonging to me. There are moments when everything is as clear as still water, and then ripples come. I have exhausted my mind and intellect.

Meera sat on her study table to think. She could not brush off something bothering her. She thought about the discoveries made by Science in the past:

Everything changed with the arrival of Albert Einstein. He discovered there was a vital link between space and time on one hand and matter on the other. Everything was intrinsically connected. He came to the realization that the universe is a big continuum of force and energy! Space is not a sheet spread out in three dimensions and time is not a linear motion but go hand in hand as space-time continuum. Matter is manifestation of the space-time complex. It is not directly pulling each other with gravitational force, but gravity itself occurs due to the space-time being wrapped like a crinkled bed sheet.

He came to a staggering discovery that all matter is basically energy in motion. And life goes on as if nothing has happened. Space ceased to be a lifeless dimension and time sprung to life. There are no objects in the world but events; no points in space but forces and waves of energy. We are in a dynamic universe of energy, vibrating at different levels. This energy is the matrix of all things seen and unseen. The pebbles I touch, the trees I see, and the people I love are adjustments of space-time; they have been reduced to conceptual field of mathematical points. I am not an individual with a physical body but a mathematical point and event in space-time! This energy condenses, beyond human comprehension, into heaviness in mountains, liquidity in water, and dimensions in objects. It is the same energy that becomes light when I see, sound when I hear, taste and smell when I taste and smell. It is sweetness in sugar, heat in fire, beauty in beautiful, formless in form, intelligence in intellect. The same continuum becomes atoms, cells, bodies, stars, and galaxies. I have become the cosmos!

More she thought about the enigmatic structure of energy and space-time, more she realized the boundary between her body and energy was becoming thinner right in front of her eyes. She felt lighter like a feather. She did not experience fear, only thrill. Eventually boundaries melted into nothingness, and everything became a radiance. She was left with nothing; nothing which was filled with everything, a brilliance of joy and laughter.

She touched the chair she was going to sit on. She sat on it, relieved she did not fall. She was glad to feel sensation of touch. A new understanding came upon her. *What made her different from a chair was the speed of vibrations.* She laughed as she realized she might as well have been that chair. She did not have an independent existence. If she stopped vibrating at the speed she was, she would become a different person, or perhaps a thing. She realized that even she was not her own, and still everything was hers. She sat there motionless, trying to unravel the mystery as to why her being was vibrating at a level that made her a person. Not just any person but the kind of person she was with her peculiar traits, personality, wishes, desires, and fears. The thought brought relief that she was part of something she could not decipher, whose existence she did not know of. Everything was been done spontaneously and effortlessly. She was been taken care of by the universe, loved and protected, as she continued to live in the bliss of ignorance. At the same time, it brought restlessness because there still remained an unsolved mystery, and her mind could not stop working till the mystery was solved.

As she was drowning in the realization that she was not a content in the field of the universe, but that she was of the basic structure of the cosmos, a wave surged in and threw her into a spasm of delight. She felt that the universe was breathing with her, through her. It was experiential, not intellectual. Her body was on the verge of breaking. A thrill was passing through every limb which gained momentum as she stepped more and more in the depth of understanding.

I am transported to eternity just by thinking like that. It is a Zen puzzle which has no end, and I come to a zero point contemplating on the structure of the universe. I have come to the edge of the mind. Space-time exists within the realm of the mind, beyond which it has no existence whatsoever. My mind cannot take me further because my intelligence is after all an effect of the cosmic intelligence. But there are times when I transcend all mental phenomenons and find myself at a place where there are no questions and no answers, only a vast space of purity. My mind gets hushed, and I experience a kind of euphoria. Language becomes inadequate, heart surrenders, and a different kind of silence prevails when I try to comprehend what this mystery is. In the deepest recess of my own heart I carry a great mystery. To access it, I have to bid goodbye to this friend of mine, mind, and enter an unknown zone and trust whatever is there. But mind is a good friend, a powerful ally, and a much powerful traitor. It has no dignity. This is the dilemma. It is not a concrete thing which I can pick and throw. It is a wave and a force which has deep hold on me.

I can look at the equation in another way: If everything is relative and changing, then where is the Absolute? In this world where everything adjusts itself to another, where pleasure and pain complement each other, where desire and fear are the creative impulses in man, there is something which needs no support; it is the absolute principle, observing the relativeness of the world. It has to be somewhere in the existing world and has to be inside me so as to make this observation possible that everything is relative. I am an awareness that observes!

In blink of an eye, Meera crossed the boundary from the known to the unknown and remembered in a flash that boundaries did not exist. They are phantoms of the mind. Known was unknown, and unknown was known. What existed was not known or unknown but one single point. *And* point cannot be divided. If she hold on to that subtle point within, from where the awareness of I arises, everything will be bestowed on her, things of this world and other worlds, and also her, for this quest is nothing but the quest of the self. This is the greatest scientific discovery.

She laughed in amusement as she reflected on her whole life was dedicated to finding the mystery of space-time, not knowing that finding the secret of the mind was the same as space-time for both were one and the same thing. She was amazed at how mind acts as a mirror and in the absence of thoughts and concepts, in moments of clear perception, it ceases to function, and the self luminous higher being flashes forth from within, as the sea of energy filled with bliss and completeness. With crystal clarity she understood the secret of space-time and the secret of mind.

Just observe an atom. It encloses huge amounts of energy within. When two atoms are smashed together, the walls enclosing space-time gets ripped and the smallness of an atom transforms into unimaginable largeness as in nuclear fission. We can experience the same results psychologically by concentrating on a single point in space-time, any point, for each and every point is the point of the Big Bang. Then, the universal hidden behind comes gushing forth from within, breaking all the boundaries of the mind and body. Mind gets dissolved and a big expanse of infinite bliss remains. Spell gets broken. Magic begins to happen.

It was an unusual day by any standard. The sun was shining bright bringing a kind of delight. Meera wanted her mentor professor to see the article she had written about the Big Bang and her ecstatic experience afterwards. Somehow, she knew those were not ordinary experiences. In fact those were not even experiences but facts staring at her face. Suddenly, she began to feel lighter and lighter till she no longer felt the gravity of the earth pulling her towards itself. To her amazement, she realized her feet were not touching the ground. She was floating few inches above the ground. Scared at first, and then she began to enjoy. How would she explain that to the professor, she came back to the house. Such a powerful feeling that the world was hers, she began to swim in the backyard pool. As she went under, she realized she had become something which existed in water as space. She was nowhere yet she was everywhere. She didn't have to breathe either. She had penetrated the fabric of space-time and found herself everywhere! A powerful wave of goodness gripped and threw her in spasm of pleasure as she struggled to come up.

How long she lay there besides the pool, she had no awareness. When she came to she went to her room up the winding stairs and called a friend who was seeing a psychologist. After she took his phone number, she fixed herself a sandwich. It was 10 o' clock in the night as she finally slept with the number on her bedside. That was the last anyone heard from her.

She vanished without leaving a trace. Some even speculated being kidnapped by aliens. Over the course of years various sightings were reported, but she was never found. Her notes and articles were found on her writing table which the police confiscated. Mystery to her disappearance remains a mystery.

THE END

≈ **26** ≈

The Final Chapter

"Reality is merely an illusion, albeit a very persistent one." — *Albert Einstein.*

People called him Krishna. He was a holy man. When or where he was born, he knew not. It all had become a memory to him, like a dream he experienced long time ago. People saw that he was a wise man; it shone in his eyes. They came from near and far for advice, listened to what he had to say. He said that the world was one; that everyone came from the same consciousness; that living in harmony and peace was the goal of life. He wanted them to understand the folly of the mind and the play of existence.

People listened. They bowed their heads in reverence. They worshipped him. They went back to their homes and fought with their spouses, with their children, with their neighbors. They chanted whatever he said, burned candles in front of his picture, made temples around him. They invented new rituals and made a religion out of him, believing they were surrendering and would reach heaven in afterlife.

Krishna's eyes were filled with tears. He felt the pain of the people and their inability to understand. He was showing them the road, and they were standing on the path chanting and praying but refusing to take a step ahead. He felt like a doctor prescribing medicine for their ailment. Instead of taking the medicine, the so-called intellectuals researched the salts that went in to make the medicine, recited the ingredients every day, but refused to take the medicine. Instead, they fought with their neighbors that their doctor was better.

Accepting his inability to communicate the greatest truth to fellow humans, Krishna retreated to the hollow space inside a banyan tree and began to live there, immersed in the glory of the universal.

Centuries passed; how many, he didn't know. On a random day, as he was meditating, he saw something glowing in the air. As he focused, which he could due to ages of spiritual living and meditation, he realized that he was seeing someone's eyes. Slowly the body manifested, and he found himself being looked upon by a person, a woman to be precise, one who appeared out of nowhere. With the powers attained through years of spiritual practice he knew in an instant what was happening. The person was Radha; she was evolving to higher dimension. She was beginning to see clearly behind the veil of her fears, desires, stories, and memories. In the complete stillness of mind, she had pierced the veil of space-time and found herself facing him in another dimension, but she was not aware of it due to certain hindrances still existing in her mind. There is the space of the world and the space of the mind; one is the space of matter and another is the space of dream, and yet there is another kind of space called transcendental space through which one can travel in between all other spaces.

He felt an impulse to help her restless soul from its torment. Her persistent inquiry combined with more and more awareness had made a potent combination which even he could not ignore. If a child is hurt in a playground, then any grown up present has to help the child. Krishna felt responsible for Radha. Her burning desire to know the reality, her powerful inquiry had rendered him powerless. *What you shall seek, you shall find.* The time had come for her to claim what was hers to begin with and pass it on to the world.

Whenever he appeared to her, it seemed to Radha that she was dreaming because of certain obstacles still in her mind. He pierced her mind and showed her the way. Her mind had become sharp enough to grasp the true meaning of life and existence. Now she didn't need him anymore. Her own awareness would lead her where she wished to go. She would live in the world as her own creation, making others who wanted to remember what had been forgotten.

The woman appeared in her dream once again after a long time.

"Who are you?" Radha asked.

"You know me as you know yourself. I am Meera." And then she disappeared in the corners of her mind.

Radha understood what had happened. As space-time complex was no longer a hindrance to Meera's movement—she had penetrated the fabric of the cosmos—she roamed the universe in abandon delight. From this dimension to that dimension as one room to another; her past had become a memory. She knew she had existed in the dimension of a book and then she could roam in any dimension, of book or otherwise. Finally she reached a mountain where she decided to live in peace for the rest of her days. Her days and nights were filled with the joy of everyday existence. She knew no hunger, thirst, or fear; only freedom, total and complete. Then one day she saw a woman appear from under a waterfall on the mountains. Meera had waited long enough for Radha, for she was Radha.

The morning arrived and Radha went for her usual morning walk, mesmerized by the seduction of the mind and its power over human beings.

———————

―――――――

"The awareness in us that knows everything

whether waking, dreaming or in deep sleep that is the "I",

The Point of the Big Bang.

It is through which we experience everything,

but which nothing else can experience.

It is through which we think through the intelligence,

but which nothing can think.

It is through which we see, hear, speak, smell, and move,

but which nothing can see, hear, speak, smell or move.

It's very essence is unbroken awareness of happiness."

―――――――